Come Close

A 30-DAY GUIDE TO
SPENDING TIME WITH GOD

LINDSEY MASTER

Every moment
OF THE DAY IS AN
OPPORTUNITY TO
BE CLOSE TO AND
TRANSFORMED BY GOD.

INTRO

week one THE BASICS OF QUIET TIME

week Two READING THE BIBLE

week Three PRAYER

week four THE STORY OF JESUS

week five WHO IS JESUS?

week six WHO ARE YOU?

BEFORE

WE BEGIN

Hey there! You are about to spend the next few weeks learning what spending time with God can look like. Some people call this a "quiet time" or "time with the Lord." You can call it anything you want. The purpose of this book is not to give you a list of rules of what you should and should not do when spending time with God. Instead, this book will offer you options to help you figure out how spending time with God works best for you. Before you start Day 1, remind yourself of a few things:

1. **Spending time with Jesus is not supposed to be boring!** The stories of the Bible are exciting — good and evil battle one another (Ephesians 6:12), dry bones come to life (Ezekiel 37:1–14), and a leader pulls out people's hair (Nehemiah 13:25). Prayer is getting to talk to God. It is a time to have a great conversation with a friend. You might find yourself bored at times, but as a whole, this time can be filled with wonder, amazement, and some crazy stories you can tell your friends.

2. **The point of this study is to spend time with God, not to check off something on a to-do list or make yourself a "better Christian."** That means it is okay if you miss a day, or two, or three. Ask a youth leader or another older Christian if they have had a quiet time every single day this year, and you'll likely find out that they've missed a few. Do your best to spend time with God daily throughout this study because you know it will build your relationship with God, not because you are trying to be "successful."

3. **Try to complete this study at the same time every day.** When you make spending time with God a regular part of your schedule rather than something you do whenever you have the time, you are more likely to do it. It might be every morning before you get ready or the last thing you do before you go to bed every night.

4. **Ask questions.** If you are having trouble understanding something, ask someone. If someone encouraged you to do this study, they might be a great person to ask! If not, consider asking any mature, trusted Christ-follower in your life. God gave us the Church (other people who follow Jesus) so that we would have helpers and mentors to guide us in our faith.

We are praying for you as you spend time with God for the next thirty days. Thank you for choosing this study to help you dig deep into God's Word.

FINDING A VERSE CAN
BE CONFUSING AT
FIRST, BUT IT GETS
much easier
with time.

READING THE BIBLE

This study will ask you to read a passage of the Bible at the beginning of each day. You can use a copy of the Bible if you have one at home. You can also download a free Bible app on your phone or search for each passage online.

Here is how to open up the Bible and find a passage. Let's use John 3:16 as an example.

1. **Find the correct book.** In our example, the book is John. At the beginning of your Bible, you will find a table of contents. Here, each book of the Bible is listed with a page number next to it, telling you where that book of the Bible begins. Go to your table of contents, and look for the book of John (do not confuse it with 1 John, 2 John, or 3 John — those are different).

2. **Once you turn to the correct book, you need to find the right chapter.** The chapter is always the first number listed before the colon. In our example of John 3:16, the chapter is 3. Chapters are always listed with big numbers in your Bible. Find the big number 3 in John.

3. **Finally, we will find the correct verse.** The verse or verses are always listed after the colon. In your Bible, the verses are listed in smaller numbers. Find verse 16 in chapter 3.

4. **Check your work.** The verse should say something similar to this: "For God loved the world in this way: He gave his one and only Son, so that everyone who believes in him will not perish but have eternal life."

Finding a verse can be confusing at first, but it gets much easier with time. Keep practicing throughout this study, and use this page as a guide if you get lost.

ONE WEEK ONE WEEK ONE WEEK
EK ONE WEEK ONE WEEK
EK ONE WEEK ONE WEEK
EK ONE WEEK ONE WEEK
EK ONE WEEK ONE WEEK
EK ONE WEEK ONE WEEK
EK ONE WEEK ONE WEEK
EK ONE WEEK ONE WEEK

THE BASICS OF

QUIET TIME

WHAT IS QUIET TIME?

READ MARK 6:31

If you regularly attend a church, you may have heard the term "quiet time" before. But what is it? *Am I supposed to just be quiet for thirty minutes?* If that were the case, you would likely not find many people having quiet times. The idea may seem mysterious, but it is actually simple. A quiet time is a set-aside time that you spend alone with God.

Christians are people who believe in and follow Jesus; another word for "Christian" is "disciple." Disciples are students who follow the teachings and actions of a leader. As disciples of Jesus, we listen to what He says and do what He does. In the Bible, we see Jesus go away by Himself, often to spend time with His Father, God. He even invites His disciples with Him to do the same (Mark 6:31a). Jesus spends time with God for many reasons, some of which may be that He loves God and wants to be near Him to rest, to receive encouragement, and to ask questions. As disciples, we can spend time with God for all the same reasons as Jesus.

So what should a quiet time look like? Really, it can look any way you want. As long as you are alone with God, you are having a quiet time. Today, you have already read a short passage of Scripture and have the opportunity to pray to God. That is a quiet time!

Throughout this study, we will look at different practices you can use while having a quiet time. Most quiet times will include at least one, if not more, of the following:

1. **Reading God's Word:** God gives us the Bible so that we can learn more about who He is and how He wants us to live. The best way to spend time with God is to get to know Him and let Him change your heart.

2. **Prayer:** Prayer is our time to talk to God, our best and most loyal friend. We can thank God, ask Him to help us or those around us, or seek answers from the One who is all-knowing.

3. **Other spiritual disciplines:** A spiritual discipline is something you can do that helps you grow closer to God. Reading the Bible and prayer are the disciplines with which you are probably most familiar. However, there are many other practices you can use, such as silence, praying Scripture, and Scripture memorization.

GOD IS BIG. HUGE. ENORMOUS. No word can describe how vast He is. There are so many things to learn about God and so many ways to experience His love. Spending time with Him can be just as vast. It can be for ten minutes or three hours. You can take a walk and pray, or you can sit in your bedroom and read. The point of quiet time is not to follow a formula but to spend time with an amazing God. Take time to figure out how and where you experience God best, and incorporate that into your time with Him.

A quiet time is a set-aside time that you spend alone with God.

THE POINT OF QUIET
TIME IS NOT TO FOLLOW
A FORMULA BUT TO
SPEND TIME WITH
an amazing God.

REFLECT REFLECT REFLECT

What questions about quiet time do you have?
Pray about those questions, and then talk to a trusted
Christian friend or adult about your questions.

_____
_____
_____
_____

Fill in the blank: I want to have a daily quiet time because...

_____
_____
_____
_____

Make a plan. What time of the day are you going
to have your quiet times? List some places you
might like to spend time with God (e.g., your
bedroom, a park, a favorite coffee shop, etc.).

_____
_____
_____
_____
_____
_____
_____
_____
_____

WHY SPEND TIME WITH GOD?

READ JOHN 15:1-8

Think about your best friend and your favorite celebrity. What do you know about each of them? What do they know about you? You should have very different answers to those questions for each person. You can know a lot about a celebrity without actually knowing them. You might know every stat of your favorite professional baseball player, yet you have no idea who they are on the inside. Likewise, they know nothing about you. On the other hand, you probably know most everything about a close friend. You have seen them at their worst and their best. You know their dreams and fears. And they know the same about you.

God already knows every single detail about us. He created us and has been beside us ever since (Psalm 139:13, Matthew 10:30). God is already the best friend we could hope for because He knows us and loves us. But we can get to know a lot about God without actually knowing Him. We can sit in church, in a youth group, or at the dinner table and hear lots of stories about God, but that does not mean we know Him deeply. Like anyone else, knowing God requires spending one-on-one time with Him. It requires talking to Him directly and not just hearing other people talk about Him.

Jesus explains this idea in our passage for today by using the image of a vine. If you can, go outside and find a vine or a tree. Take a look at how all of the parts of the vine or tree are connected. If you were to rip a leaf or branch off of that plant, what would happen to it? It might look okay for a while, but eventually, it would turn brown and wither. Without any nutrients coming in, a plant quickly dies.

Jesus is the vine from which all of life comes. Just as a leaf needs to stay connected to a vine, we must stay close to Jesus to experience true life and growth in our faith. This growth is not always obvious — oftentimes, you will not even notice that it is happening. But Jesus promises us that staying close to Him is the only way to "produce fruit." The fruit that comes from knowing Christ, sometimes known as the fruit of the Spirit, includes love, self-control, peace, patience, and faithfulness (Galatians 5:22–23). We grow in this fruit as we spend time with God, letting His Word dwell in us richly (Colossians 3:16) and being filled with the Holy Spirit (Ephesians 5:15–21). This is why we have quiet time.

Jesus is the vine where all of life comes from.

LIKE ANYONE ELSE,
KNOWING GOD
REQUIRES SPENDING
one-on-one time
WITH HIM.

REFLECT REFLECT REFLECT

Do you know a lot *about* God, or do you
know Him? What should change in your life
so that you can know Him deeply?

_____

_____

_____

_____

How close are you to the vine of Jesus? Are you attached
and growing, close but not on the vine, or far away? Explain.

_____

_____

_____

_____

The fruit of the Spirit from Galatians 5:22–23 is listed below.
Circle which fruit of the Spirit you have seen manifest in your
life lately. Then, write a prayer, thanking God for the gift of
growth, and ask Him to continue transforming you.

LOVE   JOY   PEACE   PATIENCE   KINDNESS   GOODNESS

FAITHFULNESS   GENTLENESS   SELF-CONTROL

_____

_____

_____

_____

_____

WHO IS GOD?

READ GENESIS 1:1; JOHN 1:1–5

Imagine the most beautiful place you have ever seen on earth. Maybe it is somewhere you went on vacation or a place where something amazing happened to you. The world is filled with places of beauty and adventure because it was created by a wonderful and creative God.

Christians follow the God of the Bible. In order to know God, we should start with His Word, which tells us the great story of God and His plan for the world. Just like any story, we start at the beginning—in Genesis. The very first words in the Bible tell us so much about God. The first words are: "In the beginning, God created the heavens and the earth" (Genesis 1:1). From the start, we see that the story of the Bible has one main character—God. Unlike anyone else, God has no beginning and no end. He is eternal (Hebrews 1:10–12).

God is also creative. He thought of every single plant and animal on the earth as well as all the stars and planets in the sky. He sculpted the long snout of an elephant and the microscopic parts of an atom. We also see that God is in control. In the rest of Genesis 1, we see God create the whole universe with just words. He speaks, and things appear out of nothing. All of this beautiful creation now listens to its Creator. The wind, the waters, and the earth obey His voice (Proverbs 30:4). In just one verse, the Bible reveals so much about who God is.

You might wonder why God created this universe. Was He just lonely and wanting companionship? Was He bored and seeking entertainment? No! Because He was not alone. We see a glimpse of this in Genesis 1:2, which says, "Now the earth was formless and empty, darkness covered the surface of the watery depths, and the Spirit of God was hovering over the surface of the waters." There was God, and the *Spirit of God*, and also another that John 1 calls "the Word," who we know as Jesus. All three of these beings were there at the beginning of the world. We call this trio the Trinity—Father, Son, and Holy Spirit. So, to know God is to know Jesus (His Son) and the Holy Spirit. God is never alone or in need of anything. He is self-sufficient.

God has many characteristics, which are also called attributes, that help us better comprehend God. Each time you open your Bible, you have the chance to discover a new attribute of the Lord or have a deeper understanding of the characteristics you already know. And because God created the universe and everything in it, we can look out at the world and glimpse God in new ways. For this reason, our time with the Lord should be filled with exploring God's character.

Our time with the Lord should be filled with exploring God's character.

THE WORLD IS FILLED
WITH PLACES OF BEAUTY
AND ADVENTURE BECAUSE
IT WAS CREATED BY
*a wonderful and
creative God.*

REFLECT REFLECT REFLECT REFLECT

Pick one of the characteristics of God below that you are curious about, and look up the passages that describe it. Copy your favorite of the passages below.

CHARACTERISTIC	SCRIPTURE REFERENCE
LOVING	John 3:16, Ephesians 2:4–5, 1 John 4:16
SELF-SUFFICIENT	Isaiah 40:28–31, Acts 17:24–25, Philippians 4:19
HOLY	Revelation 4:8, Leviticus 19:2, Habakkuk 1:13
SOVEREIGN	Colossians 1:17, Psalm 24:1-2, 1 Chronicles 29:11-12

_____

_____

_____

What new thing did you learn about God today, or what did you remember about God today that you already knew?

_____

_____

_____

_____

_____

Go on a walk, or find a spot to sit outside. Look around, and notice all the beautiful things God created for us to enjoy. As you are outside, pray the prayer below.

God, You made the stars and the moon, the mountains and deserts, the flowers and trees. Everything that is good and beautiful comes from You. Thank You for creating this world and for placing me in it. Help me to see Your beauty and goodness today. Amen.

THE GOSPEL

What is the gospel? It's one of those words we often hear in church but sometimes don't understand. People tend to say "gospel" often with little-to-no explanation—for example, someone might talk about the gospel of Matthew, a gospel choir, or describe something as "the gospel truth." Yet, in order to fully understand God and His plan for us, we must understand the gospel.

THE GOSPEL IS THE MOST INCREDIBLE STORY IN HISTORY. It is more romantic than any love story, more exciting than any action flick, and more dramatic than any reality show. It is a story about a God who would do anything to be close to His people. It is a tale about a King who would sacrifice everything for His kingdom. It is an adventure with a warrior who fights an enemy to save His love. And it all starts with betrayal.

God created the whole world, including the first people, Adam and Eve. God gave them every good thing inside of a beautiful garden called Eden. They could enjoy God's creation and eat from any tree around them—except the fruit from the Tree of Knowledge of Good and Evil. Adam and Eve, being tempted by an enemy of God disguised as a snake, disobeyed God and ate the forbidden fruit. This was the first sin to ever occur on earth. After that moment, sin entered the world like cancer, attacking every living thing in its path. All of God's creation is now covered in the effects of sin—plants, animals, people, and even the ground bear the curse of sin (Genesis 3:8–24, Romans 8:20–22). Further, every single human being has inherited a sin nature. We have all chosen to disobey God and attempt to control our own lives. The Bible tells us there is a consequence for our sin—death. This death is not only physical (we will all die one day) but also spiritual. Because we have turned away from God, we are separated from Him forever, and there is nothing that any of us can do on our own to fix it. Because of our sin, we are faced with a debt we can never afford to pay. Sin creates a distance between us and God, and we cannot cross that distance on our own. We cannot go to church enough, read our Bibles enough, or do enough good deeds to make up for our sin. We are helpless. However, we are not hopeless.

God loved us so much that He chose to intervene. He did not want us to be separated from Him forever, so He made a way to fix what we have broken and pay the price of our sin. God sent His Son, Jesus, to the earth to live as one of us. Jesus became the first and only person ever to walk this earth and never sin. His perfect life became the perfect sacrifice to satisfy the payment for our sin. Jesus bore our sins on the cross, dying the death we rightfully deserved (1 Peter 2:24, Isaiah 53:6). He offered Himself in our place—the innocent given for the guilty—even though it meant He would succumb to death. In doing so, He satisfied the wrath of God and removed our sins (1 John 4:10, Romans 3:25).

Jesus was buried but not for long. Three days after His death, He rose from the dead to defeat death itself. Now there is no death for those who have faith in Jesus. Instead, God offers us eternal life with Him.

There is one road to eternal life, and it is through Jesus Christ alone. Jesus offers salvation to all those who admit their sin, believe that He died on their behalf, and confess that He is the one true Lord and Savior (Romans 10:9–10). He invites us to accept this free gift and then walk along the road of life with Him, forever forgiven and trusting Him. In Him, there is freedom from sin and death; with Him, there is eternal life. That is the gospel.

His perfect life

BECAME THE PERFECT
SACRIFICE TO SATISFY THE
PAYMENT FOR OUR SIN.

REFLECT REFLECT REFLECT

Explain the gospel in your own words.

_____

_____

_____

_____

Do you believe Jesus died to save you from sin?
Why or why not?

_____

_____

_____

_____

Have you ever prayed and told Jesus that you have faith in Him? If not, and if you so feel led, write down a prayer right now, accepting the gift of the gospel in your life if you have faith. If you have told Him, write a prayer, thanking God for the gift of the gospel in your life. If you are not sure you believe, write a prayer asking God to help you understand Him more.

_____

_____

_____

_____

_____

_____

_____

_____

SEEING THE GOSPEL

God made the heavens and the earth.

(GENESIS 1:1)

We are separated from God because of our sin, and we cannot fix it.

(ISAIAH 59:2, 64:6)

We have all sinned and fallen short of God's glory.

(ROMANS 3:23)

Jesus lived a perfect life and gave His life to pay for our sins.

(2 CORINTHIANS 5:21, HEBREWS 10:14, 1 CORINTHIANS 7:23)

Jesus rose from the dead so that we can have eternal life with Him.

(JOHN 3:16)

One day, Jesus will return, and we will live with Him forever.

(REVELATION 11:15)

For God loved the world in this way: He gave his one and only Son, so that everyone who believes in him will not perish but have eternal life.

JOHN 3:16

SPIRITUAL DISCIPLINES

READ ROMANS 12:2; 1 TIMOTHY 4:7–8

Have you ever had a moment when God felt especially close? It could have been a time when you saw His beauty in nature or a time in worship when your heart felt pulled toward His. On the other hand, you may have experienced other times when you tried to understand God but felt lost or unheard. However, no matter how close or far God feels at any time, He is always with us. He never leaves or gets too busy to notice us. Because He is always by our side, every moment of the day is an opportunity to be close to and transformed by God.

This transformation happens by the power of the Holy Spirit—the same power that raised Jesus from the dead—working in us. At the same time, God also invites us to be active participants in this work by practicing spiritual disciplines. Simply put, spiritual disciplines are biblical habits—such as prayer, reading Scripture, worship, and more—that help us, as the Spirit works within us, grow deeper in our faith. Followers of Jesus practice these spiritual disciplines for many reasons.

They show our love for God: First John 5:3 says, "For this is what love for God is: to keep his commands. And his commands are not a burden." Throughout the Bible, God commands His people to know His Word and pray. When we obey these commands, it is an act of love toward God.

2. **To grow in Christlikeness:** Jesus Himself practiced spiritual disciplines. Followers of Jesus, or disciples, want to be like Jesus. The things He did should be things we do as well. Jesus often went off alone to pray, and He read from the Scriptures. He told others His story, and He quoted Scripture to overcome temptation (Luke 4:1–13). To grow in Christlikeness (thinking, acting, and talking like Jesus), we practice spiritual disciplines.

3. **To know and experience God:** When you interact with the Bible by reading, praying, or memorizing it, you learn more or are reminded about who God is. Likewise, prayer is an opportunity to draw close to God and communicate with Him.

4. **To be transformed by the Holy Spirit:** You cannot fix yourself, and spiritual disciplines alone will not magically make you Christlike. However, when we practice these spiritual disciplines because we want to be closer to God, the Holy Spirit changes us from the inside out. Second Timothy 1:7 says, "For God has not given us a spirit of fear, but one of power, love, and sound judgment." Those who have faith in Jesus have the power of the Holy Spirit inside of them that helps them grow in Christlikeness through spiritual disciplines.

Throughout this guide, you will have the opportunity to practice a new spiritual discipline each week. The purpose of each of these is closeness with God, not perfection. God doesn't ask us to say the most beautifully worded prayers but instead prayers that reflect our hearts. God does not ask us to understand every single part of the Bible fully but invites us to discover who He is day by day.

Here are the spiritual disciplines you will practice in this guide:

- Reading the Bible (you have already started this one!)
- Prayer
- Solitude
- Scripture Memorization
- Praying Scripture
- Testimony
- Sabbath Rest

SOLITUDE

Our world is loud and busy. There is always something to read, listen to, or watch that entertains and distracts. It probably feels like adults, friends, and people on social media try to tell you what to do, eat, believe, wear, and feel most of your days. In a world like that, it can be hard to cut through the noise and distractions so that we can follow Jesus and walk in obedience. This is why we need solitude. Solitude means being alone. It requires leaving behind not only people but also distractions so that you can be alone with God. Jesus often slipped away to spend time alone, knowing that He needed solitude to find rest and spend time with God the Father.

SPENDING TIME IN SOLITUDE CAN INCLUDE:

- Listening to worship music
- Journaling
- Listening to an audio Bible
- Reading the Bible
- Praying

PRACTICE:

Try to do the following:

1. Grab your Bible and your journal, too, if you use one.
2. Go outside or somewhere in your house where there are as few distractions as possible. Leave your phone and other devices somewhere else. If possible, get away from other people.

3. Sit quietly for a minute or two, enjoying the peace of silence.

4. Thank God in prayer for this time with Him, and ask Him to show Himself to you.

5. Read Psalm 23 slowly in your head.

6. Reread it slowly aloud.

7. Write down or think about what you learned about God in this passage.

8. Write down or think about how this psalm makes you feel.

9. In prayer, thank God for what He taught you, and ask Him to reveal Himself to you as the day continues.

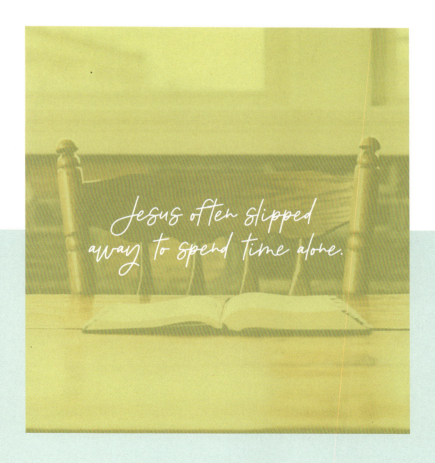

Jesus often slipped away to spend time alone.

WEEK TWO WEEK TWO WEEK TWO WEE
WEEK TWO WEEK TWO WEEK TWO WEE
WEEK TWO WEEK TWO WEEK TWO WEE
WEEK TWO WEEK TWO WEEK TWO WEE
WEEK TWO WEEK TWO WEEK TWO WEE
WEEK TWO WEEK TWO WEEK TWO WEE
WEEK TWO WEEK TWO WEE

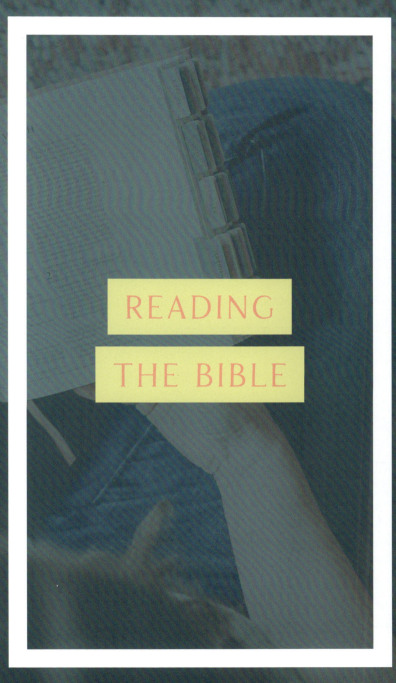

READING

THE BIBLE

WHAT IS THE BIBLE?

READ PSALM 119:103; 2 TIMOTHY 3:16–17;
EPHESIANS 6:17; JAMES 1:21–22

Think about your least-favorite class—the one you dread going to because it is confusing, complicated, or just plain boring. Have you ever had that same feeling when you open your Bible? Many of us know that we should read God's Word, but we avoid it because it is too hard to understand. Today we will look at the 5 Ws (who, what, when, where, and why) of the Bible in hopes of better understanding the Scriptures and why they are good, and maybe even fun, to read.

WHAT? The Bible is God's inerrant Word. This means that the Bible is from God, and it is completely free of error or contradiction. There is no mistake in it. The Bible is one large volume of sixty-six books. Though the Bible can feel vast and hard to understand, it helps to know the metanarrative, or overarching story, of Scripture. This can be understood in four parts: Creation, Fall, Redemption, and Restoration. These four parts (which we will unpack more tomorrow) can help us trace the story of Scripture from Genesis, the very first book, to Revelation, the very last.

The Bible is also split into two sections—the Old and New Testaments. The Old Testament covers the period of time from the creation account until four hundred years before Jesus is born, mainly following the ancient Israelites, who were God's chosen people. The New Testament, on the other hand, is all about Jesus and the early church, which forms after His death and resurrection. It covers the period from Jesus's birth until the creation of the new heaven and earth. Even though there are many sections and books, the Bible is all one big story. The story reveals who God is and who we are as well. This story tells us about how things started, how they are going, and how God will redeem it all.

WHO? The Bible is given to us by God and is all about God. The Holy Spirit inspired the authors of the Bible to write each word down. There are many characters found in God's Word—David, Abraham, Ruth, Moses, and Mary, to name a few. These were real men and women who God used to accomplish His plan of redemption. But the story of Scripture is ultimately all about Jesus—the One promised from the very beginning (Genesis 3:15) who will one day redeem all things.

WHEN? The sixty-six books of the Bible were composed at different times, starting in 1400 BC and ending in AD 95. They were written by various authors to unique audiences, but they are good for teaching anyone who wants to know God.

WHERE? Each word of the Bible is inspired by the Holy Spirit and written down by authors who generally lived in what is now the Middle East and eastern Europe. Books of the Bible were always written for a specific audience, but the truths of those words apply to anyone who follows Jesus. For example, the book of Romans is a letter that a man named Paul wrote to the church in ancient Rome—specific people living in a specific time and place. However, when Paul tells the Romans that the gospel can save anyone, that applies not just to the Romans back then but to all of us now (Romans 1:16).

WHY? The Bible is essential for our lives because it is the main way we know about God. He chooses to reveal His character and His plan to us through this book. God's Word also guides us. It shows us the path to salvation in Jesus, protects us against lies and sin, and instructs us on how life is best lived. God loves us, so He gave us a way to get to know Him, trust Him, and follow Him through the Bible.

THE BIBLE IS GIVEN TO
US BY GOD AND IS
all about God.

REFLECT REFLECT REFLECT

What is something new you learned about the Bible today?

_____

_____

_____

_____

_____

Look back at Psalm 119:103.
Why would God's Word be "sweeter than honey"?

_____

_____

_____

_____

_____

Make a list of what makes it hard for you to study
Scripture. Then, ask God to help you with each of those
struggles as you continue this study.

My Struggle with Reading the Bible	Prayed?

CAN I TRUST

THE BIBLE?

We live in a world of information. You can find out pretty much anything about anyone instantaneously with the push of a button. With all of this data available, it can be difficult to figure out what we can trust and what we cannot. If you question whether or not the Bible is true, you are not alone. Many faithful Christians ask that same question, and it does not make God angry or scared. Sometimes, we think we have to have blind faith to follow Jesus, but He never asks for that. Jesus performed countless miracles on earth *so that* people would know He really was the Son of God. God gave us the Bible *so that* we would know Him more. Curiosity is given to us by God *so that* we would search for Him, and when we have hearts that truly long to know God, He always reveals Himself. Below are answers to some of the most frequently asked questions about the Bible's reliability. If you continue to have questions, search for the answers. Talk to a trusted pastor, family member, or adult who loves Jesus, and see if they can help you along the way.

How do we know who wrote the Bible and that everything in it actually happened?

The Bible depicts actual events with real people. Just like any other ancient occurrence, we can look to historians and archaeologists to find the truth. Stories of the Old Testament were passed down for generations through oral history or written by educated scribes. These authors were well-known to those around them because they were often leaders, prophets, or missionaries in the community.

In addition to the biblical authors, there were historians, like a man named Josephus, who lived in and wrote about the ancient world. The writings of these ancient historians line up with what the Bible says happened. These historians, as well as government records, serve as evidence of the events in the Bible taking place. Today, archaeologists find artifacts of ancient civilizations and study them to learn about ancient culture. They have found many manuscripts of the books of the Bible that are all essentially the same, as well as the remains of specific locations the Bible mentions.

Further, Scripture is self-authenticating, which means that the Word of God itself shows that it was formed by God. Old Testament prophecies come true in the New Testament through the life and death of Jesus. God promised Abraham that his family would bless all the nations. When Jesus, who was a descendent of Abraham (Matthew 1:1–17), died and rose again, He made a way for all people to be free from sin and death, fulfilling that promise. The way that all of the books of the Bible weave together to tell one big story shows us there had to be one great Author behind it all.

Why are there different versions of the Bible if it is all the same book? Do some versions have it wrong?

English was not the first language of any biblical book because it did not exist until after these books were composed. The Old Testament was written in ancient Hebrew and later translated into Koine Greek, while the New Testament was written in Koine Greek. So, for English speakers to be able to read God's Word today, it had to be translated.

These ancient languages can be difficult to translate because the sentences are structured differently than in modern English. Translators also must decide whether or not to use a literal translation, where scholars translate the word into an English word with an equivalent meaning, or a dynamic translation, where scholars translate the meaning or message of a word into an equivalent word or phrase in English. Some translations, like the King James Version, were written a long time ago, so they may tend to sound more dated than current versions, such as the Christian Standard Bible. There are numer-

THROUGH PRAYER AND
PERSEVERANCE, WE CAN
TRUST IN GOD'S WORD AS
*it transforms our
hearts and minds.*

ous translations of the Bible, but the same message is clear in each major translation. You might see differences in word choice between versions but not a change in the doctrine (i.e., major beliefs). Trustworthy translations include, but are not limited to, the CSB, NIV, ESV, NLT, and NASB.

Does the Bible apply to me even though it was written thousands of years ago?

The Bible was written a long time ago for audiences who lived in a far different culture from ours. Because of this, the Bible can sometimes be confusing for us because we do not understand the metaphors that biblical authors used or how they viewed certain things. For example, Jesus talks about separating the wheat from the chaff. This was an idea that anyone living in first-century Jerusalem would understand, but who knows what chaff is today? Not very many people. Part of studying Scripture is understanding the historical context in which Scripture was written. If you look in a commentary or at the notes of a study Bible (which are always great resources to have), you will figure out that Jesus is talking about removing an inedible husk, the chaff, from a crop in order to get to the edible wheat.

Even though we are not the original audience for these books, these books are still essential for our understanding of God. We might not understand the concept of chaff, but the meaning behind Jesus's words still applies to us. With this analogy, Jesus taught that one day, God will separate the believers from those who have rejected the gospel. That was true when the book of Matthew was written and is still true today.

Ultimately, Christ-followers choose to trust in the Bible for the same reason we trust in the gospel—faith. As we grow in faith, the Holy Spirit inside of us can help us understand the value and meaning of Scripture. Through prayer and perseverance, we can trust in God's Word as it transforms our hearts and minds.

THE STORY OF SCRIPTURE

READ GENESIS 2:4–3:24; COLOSSIANS 1:15–22; REVELATION 21:1–4

Once upon a time, there was a beautiful kingdom created by a powerful king who ruled with justice and kindness. Everything in the land was good, and everyone was happy. One day, a dark cloud appeared over the kingdom, bringing with it an evil warlock who hated the king and his subjects. The warlock lied to the people of the land and tricked them into believing the king was mean and cruel rather than merciful and good. They overthrew the king and took control of the kingdom for themselves, and the dark cloud of the warlock spread over the entire kingdom, plunging everyone into darkness. The subjects, realizing their mistake in overthrowing the king, cried out in misery. The king's son, out of love for his kingdom, raced out of the castle, sword in hand, and defeated the evil warlock, restoring peace and prosperity to the kingdom forever. The end.

Most of us grow up surrounded by fairytales. As kids, we pretend to be knights slaying dragons or princesses meeting their perfect prince. We feel pulled toward myths where great battles are fought, good defeats evil, and true love prevails. We are drawn to these stories because they reflect the story written from the beginning of time revealed to us through the Bible.

THE STORY OF SCRIPTURE CONSISTS OF FOUR ACTS:

1. **Creation:** God created the heavens and the earth, and everything in them was good.

2. **Fall:** Adam and Eve listened to the enemy's lies and chose to sin. Sin entered the world and now separates us from God.

3. **Redemption:** Jesus came down from heaven and lived a perfect life in order to be a sacrifice for our sins. He took on our punishment to restore our relationship with God.

4. **Restoration:** One day, Jesus will return, and a new heaven and earth will be formed. God will bring back a world free from sin, just like the garden of Eden before the sin of Adam and Eve. There will be no more death, disease, or tears.

It takes the entire Bible to explain this story. Creation and the Fall start in the first few chapters of Genesis, and in Genesis 3:15, we see a first glimpse of the Redemption to come—what God has always planned for His people. We also see what our final Restoration will ultimately look like at the end of the last book of Revelation. As we look through God's Word, we can see these four acts of the story unfold from Genesis to Revelation but also over and over again through each story we read.

The one thing that remains true in all four parts of this story is that God is in control and works for His glory and our good. He creates, and it is good. We fall, but He loves us still, so much that He comes to us to redeem us and restore our relationship with Him. And He will one day bring an end to all the pain sin causes. God is always at work, and we get to reap the benefits of His labor. No part of this story is ours—we do not create, we do not redeem, and we do not restore. We are His creation, redeemed by His Son, and are restored by God.

WE ARE HIS CREATION,
REDEEMED BY HIS
SON, AND ARE

restored by God.

REFLECT REFLECT REFLECT

How does the story of Scripture change the
way you might read the Bible?

_____

_____

_____

_____

_____

_____

_____

If God does all the work on our behalf, what is our role in
a relationship with Him? (Read Galatians 5:13 for a clue.)

_____

_____

_____

_____

_____

_____

How do you feel about God, knowing that He created you,
died for you, and offers you eternal life?

_____

_____

_____

_____

_____

_____

_____

HOW DO I READ THE BIBLE?

READ PSALM 119:105; ACTS 8:26-39

Have you ever tried to find your way in the dark? On your own, you will likely trip and stumble, unsure where to go and unable to find your way. You need a light to guide you, to help you see. The same is true for each of us in our daily lives. We need a source of spiritual light—something to guide us in this dark world. Thankfully, we are not left alone in this task.

God has given us His Word to guide us through each and every part of our lives. In Psalm 119:105, we learn that God's Word is a lamp for our feet and a light for our path. Just as a lamp brightens a room, the Bible illuminates our path through this world. Instead of walking in darkness, the Bible equips us to walk in the light of Christ.

However, sometimes studying the Bible can feel... confusing. If you feel lost or confused as you open your Bible, you are not alone. In fact, in today's reading, we learn about a man who tried to read Scripture but ran into some confusion along the way. Acts 8:26–39 tells the story of a royal official from Ethiopia who was searching the Scriptures, specifically the book of Isaiah. However, this man couldn't understand the words he read or how to apply them to his life. At that exact moment, one of Jesus's disciples named Philip came along. Philip had been carried there by the Holy Spirit with the mission of helping the Ethiopian man understand and believe. And finally, because of the Holy Spirit's work, the Ethiopian man began to understand what he was reading! After Philip shared the gospel with him, the man asked to be baptized. Then, he went on his way, rejoicing — no longer confused but now walking in the light.

Sometimes, we can feel like the Ethiopian man. Perhaps we know we should read the Bible, but we just cannot seem to understand what it is trying to tell us. When we feel this way, we need not grow discouraged, for God has not left us alone in the task. Like the Ethiopian man, God has given us Someone to help us understand His Word — the Holy Spirit.

SO, HOW CAN WE READ OUR BIBLES IN LIGHT OF THE HOLY SPIRIT? HERE ARE A FEW TIPS:

1. **Before you open your Bible, pray.** Ask that God would use His Holy Spirit to reveal Himself to you. Such a simple prayer can help us posture our hearts before the Lord as we invite the Holy Spirit into our time in the Word.

2. **Then, open your Bible and start reading.** If you find you still do not understand, do not be afraid to ask questions. You can write your questions down, pray, and dig deeper to try to gain understanding. You can also reach out to other followers of Jesus—whether that is a group of friends, a mentor, or a youth pastor—and read the Bible together.

3. **After reading, try to summarize the passage.** When you can explain the Bible to yourself, you are more likely to remember its meaning so that the truth stays with you.

4. **Next, ask yourself:** *What does this passage teach me about God? And how does this passage change the way I think or live?* The Bible is all about God, so we can search for

who He is in each verse. The Bible is also meant to transform our hearts and then our actions, so ask yourself how you might live differently because of God's Word.

6. **Finally, end your time in God's Word with prayer.**
   Pray that the Holy Spirit would continue to work in you, transforming your heart in light of what you read and helping you glorify God. As you go about your day, you can remember that God will always be faithful to finish the good work that He has started in you (Philippians 1:6).

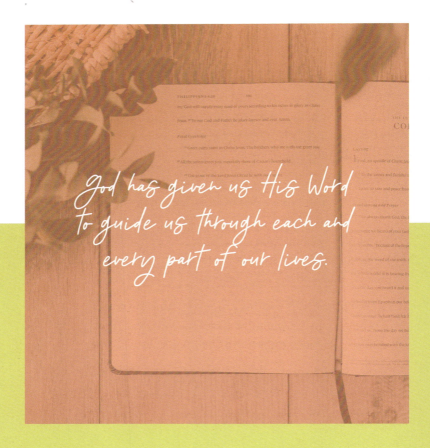

God has given us His Word to guide us through each and every part of our lives.

REFLECT REFLECT REFLECT REFLECT

Ready to practice reading God's Word? Start with prayer, then read Matthew 9:1–8 and answer the following questions.

Write a one-sentence summary of the passage.

_____

_____

_____

What does this passage teach you about God?
Think about the characteristics of God you saw in
this passage—for example, look at how Jesus acted
and how others responded.

_____

_____

_____

How does this change the way you think or live?
Do you see God differently, or do you want to change
the way you act to be more like Jesus?

_____

_____

_____

Finally, end in prayer, thanking God for what you read and
asking Him to continue to work in you.

_____

_____

_____

_____

UNDERSTANDING THE OLD TESTAMENT

**READ GENESIS 3:13–15, 15:1–6;
2 SAMUEL 7:8–16; MALACHI 4**

There are moments in life when things just start to click—when you learn how to ride a bike, when you swing a bat and actually hit the ball, or when all the jumbled letters on a page become words you can read. The Old Testament is an assortment of ideas and stories that may seem like a mess of letters that do not go together. However, once we learn how to read it, it can transform into beautiful words that string together to reveal an amazing story full of twists, turns, and wild events. Did you know that in the Old Testament there are stories about:

- Spies hiding behind enemy lines to report back to their army (Joshua 2:1–7)

- Brothers murdering, stealing from, and kidnapping one another (Genesis 4:1–12, 27:1–38, 37:12–28)

- Women boldly trusting in God (Joshua 2:8–14; Ruth 3:5–9; Esther 7:3–4)

Remember, the Bible is all about God and His plan. The Old Testament reveals how God created the world, His people, and His kingdom. In the beginning, God made every single thing in the universe, including people. Quickly, Adam and Eve broke their relationship with God through sin, causing the fall of God's creation. But, while God explains the consequences for sin, God also makes a promise filled with hope. He tells the serpent who deceived Eve that, one day, one of Eve's descendants will strike his head. While the serpent will injure this future descendant by striking His heel, the strike to the serpent's head will be a final, fatal blow. This is God's first promise that the serpent will one day be fully and finally defeated. The rest of the Old Testament builds upon this promise as God's people wait for this future descendant of Eve who will defeat the enemy and make all things right. This future descendant of Eve is sometimes referred to as the Second Adam. Where the first Adam failed, God promises that the Second Adam will come to save God's people and reign victorious. Today, we know this man as Jesus.

From Genesis 3:15 and on, the Old Testament follows the family lineage of the first Adam as he leaves the garden and humanity experiences the far-reaching effects of sin. Out of this lineage, we find a man named Abram. God chooses Abram to become the first of His chosen people. Even though he and his wife are old—over one hundred years of age—and barren, God promises to make a great nation from Abram's descendants. God says that from this family, all of the nations of the world will be blessed. The Second Adam—the one God promised in Genesis 3:15—will come through Abram's family.

Abram, who is now renamed Abraham, does indeed have a son, and he has sons, and they have sons, and on and on until the family grows into the nation of Israel. One of the greatest kings of Israel is David, himself a descendant of Abraham and the first Adam. To David, God makes another promise. The Second Adam—the Savior—will come from David's line of descendants and will sit on an eternal throne as King.

The nation of Israel is God's chosen people, not because they are better than anyone else but because God chooses them. In fact, we see Israel fail to obey God time after time as we study the Old Testament. Just like the first Adam, every one of the Israelites turns away from God and serves themselves. By the last book of the Old Testament, Israel seems doomed. They fail to follow God, and the Second Adam has not yet arrived. God's people are separated from Him, and they cannot fix their broken hearts. We are the same. No matter how hard we try, we all sin and are hopeless for a solution on our own.

If this were the end of the Bible, this story would be a tragedy, and we would all be doomed. Thankfully, we have more to the story coming. The Second Adam is on the way. The Old Testament ends with the hope that Jesus is coming to save His people—for this was the plan all along.

This is God's first promise that the serpent will one day be fully and finally defeated.

REFLECT REFLECT REFLECT

How does the Old Testament show
us our need for a Savior?

_____

_____

_____

_____

_____

_____

What is something new you learned about
the Old Testament today?

_____

_____

_____

_____

_____

_____

How do you feel knowing that God chose His people not
because they were good but just because He loved them?

_____

_____

_____

_____

_____

_____

_____

_____

UNDERSTANDING
THE NEW TESTAMENT

READ MATTHEW 1; JOHN 1:1–18

Can you remember a time you had to wait for a new season of a show or book in a series to release? There is a tension that builds up within you, causing your heart to feel tight and your brain foggy as you wait to know how the story is going to end. *Did he make it out of the car crash? Will she actually tell him how she feels?*

This is how the Israelites felt for four hundred years. Yes, you read that right—four hundred years. The Old Testament ends on the biggest cliffhanger in history. God promises that a Savior is coming to fix all that sin broke, but the world seems as dark as ever. After the last book of the Old Testament is written, there is a period of silence—four hundred years in which God sends no prophets. This is the calm before the storm. We might miss this when we flip straight from the book of Malachi to Matthew in our Bibles because those two books are only one page apart, but the Israelites certainly felt the pain of waiting. Maybe you have felt that same way as you waited for God to do something in your life. Perhaps there is someone sick you want to be better, a friendship you desperately want to mend, or broken family relationships you want to heal. You may pray for those things and yet feel like God is silent.

The first book in the New Testament, the book of Matthew, starts, strangely enough, with a genealogy. The family line of one man is traced back all the way to two notable men from the Old Testament—Abraham and David. This may seem like a boring way to start a book, but it would have been incredibly exciting for first readers of this book. The One they have been waiting hundreds of years for is finally here. Emmanuel is born. God has come to live with us. God—who existed since before the beginning of time, who made all of life, who is light itself, who drives out the darkness in our hearts—is lying in a manger, and His name is Jesus. God always keeps His promises. He proves that to us when Jesus is born to save us from our sins.

The first four books of the New Testament—Matthew, Mark, Luke, and John—are called the Gospels, and they are all about the life, death, and resurrection of Jesus. They tell stories of how Jesus acts and speaks on earth so that we can better know the One who loves us so much that He was willing to die for us. When we read the Gospels, we learn more about Jesus's life so that we can understand Him better. We also see an example of how to live a God-glorifying life so that we can replicate it. The author of the book of Luke wrote a sequel to his Gospel. That sequel is called Acts. This book continues the story after Jesus is resurrected; it shows us what happened to the earliest Christ followers and how they built the first communities of Christians, called churches. These five books—the four Gospels and Acts—are historical. They tell us about events that truly happened with people who really lived.

The rest of the New Testament books (except the last book of Revelation) are called the Epistles, which means "letters." They are notes that the leaders of the first churches wrote to other Christians or churches. If you look at the beginning of most of these books, you will see a normal greeting from a letter; typically, the author tells you who he is and to whom he is writing (look at Ephesians 1:1 for an example). These books help us understand how to live life with Jesus. The last book, Revelation, tells us how one day, Jesus will return to restore all things. At this future time, Jesus will end the power of sin and death once and for all. Everything that is broken will be made whole.

When we combine the Old and New Testaments, we see two chapters of one tale. God created a world that was broken by sin. The people, incapable of fixing what they broke, awaited a Savior. That Savior arrived and died in our place. Now, we can live close to God and obey His commands with the help of the Holy Spirit until one day when Jesus will return and end the pain of sin and death forever.

These books help us understand how to live life with Jesus.

REFLECT REFLECT REFLECT REFLECT

Summarize what the Bible is about in your own words.
Think about the Old and New Testaments
and how they fit together.

_____
_____
_____
_____
_____
_____
_____

How do we know God keeps His promises?

_____
_____
_____
_____
_____

Read Deuteronomy 31:8. What promise does
God make to us in this passage?

_____
_____
_____
_____
_____
_____
_____
_____

SCRIPTURE MEMORIZATION

This book of instruction must not depart from your mouth; you are to meditate on it day and night so that you may carefully observe everything written in it. For then you will prosper and succeed in whatever you do.

JOSHUA 1:8

My son, don't forget my teaching, but let your heart keep my commands; for they will bring you many days, a full life, and well-being.

PROVERBS 3:1–2

You consume a lot of information. You have to learn facts for school, information about your friends and family, and skills for sports, playing music, or dance. On top of that, you see a lot of information from social media and the internet every day. With all of these facts swimming around in our minds, it can be hard to remember God's Word. Sometimes you might read your Bible, and the moment you end your quiet time, forget what you have just read!

God asks us to not only read the Bible but "meditate on it day and night" (Joshua 1:8) and "let your heart keep my commands" (Proverbs 3:1–2). We can follow this command through Scripture memorization. You might not always have your Bible by your side, but you can take God's truth wherever you go when it lives in your heart. Memorizing Scripture helps you accomplish this.

PRACTICE:

This week, try to memorize the following passage. You can do this by:

1. Repeating the passage out loud.
2. Writing down the passage multiple times.
3. Listening to the passage on audio on repeat.

Take a few minutes each day to memorize this passage until you have it down by heart. When you are having a hard time, this passage will be written on your heart to remind you of God's truth.

> Love consists in this: not that we loved God,
> but that he loved us and sent his Son to be
> the atoning sacrifice for our sins.
>
> ### 1 JOHN 4:10

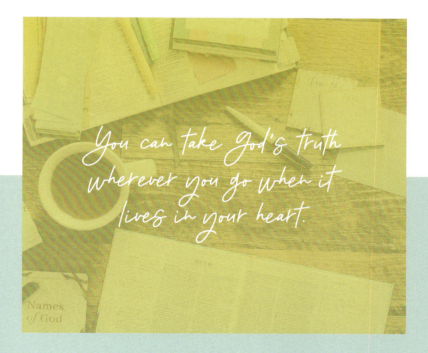

You can take God's truth wherever you go when it lives in your heart.

WEEK THREE WEEK THREE WEEK THREE W
EK THREE WEEK THREE WEEK THREE W
EK THREE WEEK THREE WEEK THREE W
EK THREE WEEK THREE WEEK THREE W
EK THREE WEEK THREE WEEK THREE W
EK THREE WEEK THREE WEEK THREE W
EK THREE WEEK THREE WEEK THREE W
EK THREE WEEK WE

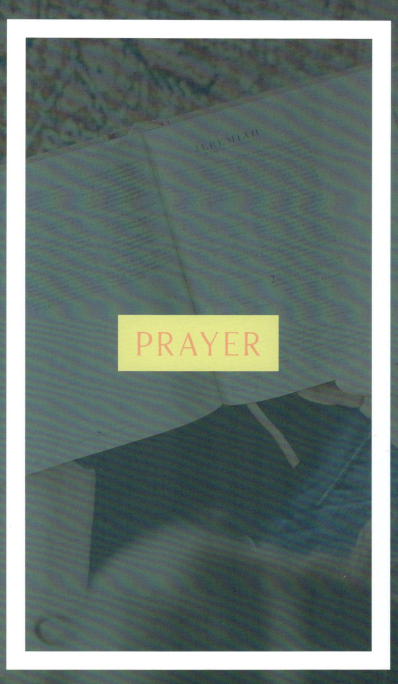

PRAYER

WHAT IS PRAYER?

READ LUKE 5:17–26; 1 JOHN 5:14–15

A girl lays on a small bed inside a cramped hospital room, listening to the beeps and sighs of machines behind her. A doctor knocks on the door, looking to fix what is broken. He has already seen her chart and knows just what to do but still sweetly asks, "What's wrong?" She pours out all the pain she feels, and then she waits—waits for the doctor to say or do something to take away all that bothers her.

Like this girl, most of us go straight to a doctor when we are sick. Once we tell him where the pain is, we trust that he will figure out the rest and tell us how to get better. But what do we do when we have pain that a doctor could never fix? We might feel lonely, overwhelmed, confused, hurt, or angry. Perhaps there is someone in our life who is suffering immensely, and we do not know how to help. Or maybe there is a situation in the world that is scary and sad, and we feel too small to do anything about it.

In today's reading, we learn about a group of friends who feel this way when they decide to take their friend to see Jesus. Their friend is paralyzed—unable to move on his own. His friends know they cannot heal him, so they pick him up on a mat and carry him to the place where Jesus is teaching. But, when they arrive, there are so many people crammed into the building that they cannot get near Jesus. So, they get creative. Climbing up onto the roof of the house, the friends rip apart the roof until they make a hole big enough to drop the paralytic down. Seeing their faith, Jesus immediately heals their friend, and the man who was once paralyzed walks home, glorifying God.

This story paints a beautiful picture of prayer. Prayer is admitting we are helpless to the One we trust to have all the help we need. The friends in this story had no power to heal their paralyzed friend. Completely helpless, they knew there was nothing they could do to fix this man's body. So many of us view helplessness as an embarrassment—something we should never admit. We hide our weaknesses and pretend that we are in control. But being helpless is part of being human. We cannot change our hearts or the hearts of those around us that have been darkened by sin.

There is only one doctor who can truly heal all the hurts in our lives—Jesus. We must go to Him, admitting our inability to fix our sin and the sin of others. But on top of admitting helplessness, we must also have faith. Ole Hallesby writes, "Helplessness united with faith produces prayer. Without faith, our helplessness would be only a vain cry of distress in the night" (Hallesby, 28). Crying out for help is useless unless there is someone to hear us. Jesus is alive. He died and rose from the grave to eternal life, and He promises that He is always near. We believe in a living God who turns His head toward those who cry out to Him. Prayer is an act of faith as we trust Jesus to hear us and help us.

You might feel like there is a certain way, time, or structure to pray, and that could make prayer feel intimidating. However, we see all kinds of different prayers in the Bible—prayers for help and protection; prayers in praise of God; and prayers in frustration, desperation, and joy. There is no one way or time to pray. We pray any time we realize our helplessness, running to our God, who is powerful enough to heal all wounds. And anytime we pray, we have the confidence that God hears us.

Everyone gathered around Jesus was astounded at this miracle that took place and the way Jesus responded—even the scribes and the

Pharisees, who were at first skeptical. The scribes and the Pharisees, an elite group of religious leaders, thought they had faith and God all figured out, but they misunderstood who God is and what He wants from us. Tomorrow, we will see how they chose to pray and what we can learn from their mistakes.

Prayer is admitting we are helpless to the One we trust to have all the help we need.

REFLECT REFLECT REFLECT REFLECT

In your own words, what is prayer?

_____

_____

_____

_____

_____

_____

_____

_____

_____

What has prayer looked like in your life up to this point
(when, where, how, how often do you pray)?

_____

_____

_____

_____

_____

How has your view of prayer changed?

_____

_____

_____

_____

_____

_____

_____

_____

HOW *NOT* TO PRAY

READ MATTHEW 6:5–8; LUKE 18:9–14

Have you ever had a group project in school where one person did not do any of the work but took all the credit for the grade? Or a teammate who never practiced or played well but acted like they were the reason you won a game? It can be infuriating to listen to someone who has not contributed steal the glory away from others who did put in the effort. In today's reading, Jesus reveals a group of religious leaders who were stealing away God's glory as they pretended their good works earned God's favor.

In Jesus's time, the Pharisees think they are a really big deal to God. They wear all the right clothes, go to the temple (their version of church), sacrifice animals, tell everyone else how to live the right way, and speak long and elegant prayers. They work hard to earn God's favor and think everyone should look up to them because of how holy they are. When the Pharisees pray, they do not feel helpless but powerful. They believe that God listens to them because of how good they are, and they pray loudly so that others know it as well. We know, though, that true prayer comes not from our goodness but our helplessness.

Jesus explains that the Pharisees' version of prayer is not what God wants because it is all about them. The Pharisees show off in prayer rather than submit to God. They try to control God rather than allowing Him to guide their steps. The sinner is truly praying because he admits his helplessness and asks for God's help, while the religious Pharisee uses prayer as an excuse to look down on others. It seems like the Pharisees treat God like Santa Claus—if they are good, they will get the gifts they want. But God is our Father who gives good gifts because He loves us and not because we work for it. The Pharisees thought they had to say the right words for God to hear them, yet prayer is not about our words but our hearts. Jesus lived a perfect life in our place, so we do not have to prove that we are good enough to be heard by God. Jesus steps in to be our "enough." Prayer is not about earning God's favor but submitting ourselves to His will and remembering His power to defeat any enemy in our lives.

Remember what prayer truly is—admitting we are helpless and running in faith to God for rescue. Prayer begins in our hearts and pours out through our words to the Lord. As believers, our hearts are transformed, and this transformation is reflected not only in the choices we make but also in the words we say. And yet, sometimes prayer is so deep within our hearts that we do not even have words to express it. The Pharisees might say that a prayer without words is not prayer, but God says any cry to Him will be heard, even if our lips stay still. There is no perfect prayer but only imperfect words to a perfect God. God delights in our prayers simply when they come from a love for Him.

True prayer comes not from our goodness but our helplessness.

Prayer begins in our hearts

AND POURS OUT
THROUGH OUR WORDS
TO THE LORD.

ISAIAH 59:19

REFLECT REFLECT REFLECT

Compare the Pharisees' view of prayer with God's.

How the Pharisees Define Prayer	How God Defines Prayer

How can you change from praying with
just words to praying with your heart?

_____

_____

_____

_____

Have you prayed to God for salvation with just your
words and not your heart? If so, or if you have never
prayed for salvation and want to right now, write
a prayer to God admitting that you are helpless in
your sin but have faith in His power to save.

_____

_____

_____

_____

_____

_____

THE LORD'S PRAYER

READ MATTHEW 6:9–13

Words are hard. Sometimes we have so much to say but cannot find the words to express how we feel. There are other times when we think we should say something but are not sure of exactly the right thing to say. Yesterday we learned that God is not interested in perfect prayer but prayer that comes from the heart. Even if we know that is true, prayer can still seem intimidating because we are not sure where to start. Thankfully, we have the perfect example in Jesus for how life is to be lived and prayers are to be prayed.

Many refer to the passage today as "The Lord's Prayer" or "The Jesus Prayer." You might even say a version of this prayer at your church. These words are not magic or special; saying them means nothing if they do not come from within our hearts. However, Jesus gives us these words as a guide for how we can all pray. This is why Jesus does not say, "pray this exactly," but instead instructs us to "pray like this" or, in other words, "pray in this way." This prayer reveals four ways for us to pray to God.

/ **Praise God:** Jesus starts His prayer by praising God for who He is: "Our Father in heaven, your name be honored as holy." God is in heaven sitting on a throne as King, and the world should honor Him as the ruler and Creator of heaven and earth. When we pray, we should take time to praise God and thank Him for all that He is and has done for us.

2. **Submit to God:** After praising God, Jesus prays, "Your kingdom come. Your will be done on earth as it is in heaven." With these words, Jesus is modeling submission to God and God's perfect will. To submit to God is simply to recognize that He is more powerful and wise than we could ever be. For this reason, we trust His plans, and we live according to His desires.

3. **Ask:** Next, Jesus prays for daily bread. Each morning, we can awaken and ask God to give us all we need. This reminds us that God is ultimately in control of our lives and wants to guide us each step of the way.

4. **Confess:** Finally, Jesus asks God to forgive us our debts—our sins against Him. We should confess to God when we sin. This is not so that we feel guilty or shameful, but so we can offer the darkest parts of ourselves to Him and remember we are forgiven and loved.

In the Lord's Prayer, Jesus is reminding us that God is the focus of our prayers. We should recognize the character of God and submit ourselves to His will before boldly bringing our requests to Him and asking Him to empower us to live upright and Godly lives. When we center our hearts on Christ in prayer, our focus turns from ourselves to our Savior. Our will becomes subject to His will, and our prayers become a recognition of our trust in His sovereignty and our dependence upon His might. So when we pray for strength, we are really praying for God's strength to fill us. When we pray for healing, we are really praying for God to fix what is broken through His Almighty power. When we pray for deliverance over evil, we are asking for the Spirit to put to death the deeds of the flesh. Prayer should remind us that God is sovereign and we are not.

Follow the model of the Lord's Prayer as you write
your own prayer, using the prompts to guide you.
Pray this prayer after you write it.

PRAYER PROMPTS

What is something you love about God or learned about Him this week? Praise Him for who He is or what He has done.

Thank God for what He has done for you or someone you know.

What is something you or someone else needs today? Ask God to provide.

What sin has God revealed in you this week? Confess your sin to God, and ask Him to change you from the inside out.

HOW GOD ANSWERS PRAYERS

Adults can ask a lot from us sometimes. You may be in the middle of homework, relaxing, or just getting home for the day when your parents need you to clean the kitchen, do the laundry, or pick up the living room. But can you imagine if your mom or dad looked over at you at dinner and asked if you could make some french fries appear on their plate out of thin air? You would stare at them in disbelief, wondering if they needed medical attention. In today's reading, Jesus's mother, Mary, does not ask for fries, but she does make a pretty extraordinary request of her Son.

Jesus is relaxing at a wedding with friends when Mary alerts Him to a problem. The bride's family has run out of wine, and the festivities still have a long way to go. This is a major embarrassment for the family because it gives the impression that they cannot properly celebrate their daughter. They need more wine. Mary tells Jesus the need, asks the servants to follow Jesus's commands, and then walks away. She does not ask Jesus how He will provide, but the moment she makes her request, she immediately trusts that He will do something. There is no way she could have known that Jesus was going to fill jars full of dirty water and miraculously turn that water into wine, yet she boldly asks for what she needs, for she knows that Jesus loves and came into the world to fix what is broken. Ultimately, we know that Jesus deals with the much larger problem of sin by dying on the cross. His own body would eventually be broken that ours could one day be made whole.

Jesus not only gives Mary what she asks for but gives it in abundance. He makes more than enough wine for the wedding, and based on the headwaiter's response in verses 9–10, this new wine tastes better than what they had before. This is truly a miraculous answer to Mary's request, proving Jesus's ability to provide.

However, just like Mary did not expect wine to come from dirty water, we cannot expect God to always answer our prayers in a specific way. When we try to control God, we miss out on the point of prayer, which is intimacy with Him. We can always trust God to hear us but cannot expect to know exactly how God will act. Furthermore, in this story, Mary does not know exactly when Jesus is going to help because she walks away right after making her request. Scripture does not tell us how quickly Jesus responded — perhaps He acted instantaneously, or perhaps He took His time. However, even though Mary did not completely understand how Jesus would provide or how quickly He would act, she demonstrated trust in Him when she told the servants to "do whatever he tells you" (verse 5). Likewise, we can do the same. We can present our requests to God and trust Him to act in His own perfect timing and ways.

God wants us to come to Him in prayer and sometimes asks us to wait patiently. God's ways are not our ways. One way we can look at this is by thinking about an airplane. Have you ever seen an airplane fly above you and wondered what the passengers on board see? From their vantage point, they can see everything that surrounds you: all the fields, cities, roads, train tracks, everything for miles and miles. You, on the other hand, can only see what's right around you. Similarly, God can see everything in the world that has happened, is happening, and will happen. He is outside of time. We, on the other hand, only see what is right in front of us. We cannot know all of God's ways, so we choose to trust that He does hear us and will act at the right moment.

WE CAN PRESENT OUR
REQUESTS TO GOD AND
trust Him to act
IN HIS OWN PERFECT
TIMING AND WAYS.

REFLECT REFLECT REFLECT

Read Matthew 7:9–11. Why does God
give good gifts to His children?

_____

_____

_____

_____

Read Luke 18:1–8. Why did the judge listen to the widow?
What does this passage tell us about how
and how often we should pray?

_____

_____

_____

_____

Read Luke 22:42. Jesus prays these words the night
before His death on the cross. Did God answer this
prayer? Why or why not? What does this teach
us about how God answers prayer?

_____

_____

_____

_____

_____

_____

_____

_____

_____

PRAYING IN
THE HOLY SPIRIT

**READ MATTHEW 28:19; EPHESIANS 6:18;
ROMANS 8:26–27**

There is a term used often by the Church that many people struggle to understand. This term is "the Trinity." Like a triangle has three sides, the Trinity has three persons. These three persons together make up the Godhead.

But wait, you might be thinking, *doesn't the Bible say that we serve one God, not three?* Yes. Are there three persons that make up the one God we serve? Also yes. This is the mystery of the Trinity—God the Father, God the Son, and God the Holy Spirit. Each of these is distinct and yet one. God the Father is in heaven; His Son came down to earth to live among us, die for our sins, resurrect, and then return to heaven; and the Spirit dwells inside those who follow Jesus. The Trinity has always been and always will be—the Trinity has no beginning or end.

We see the presence of the Trinity in Scripture. In the beginning, before the world was formed, the Spirit of God hovered over the waters (Genesis 1:1–2). That is the Holy Spirit. The Word, Jesus, was there as well (John 1:1–3). Throughout the Old Testament, there are appearances of God the Father, God the Son, and God the Holy Spirit. At the beginning of the New Testament, God the Son comes down to earth as a baby named Jesus. He lives a perfect life and dies for us on the cross. Three days after His death, He is resurrected and with His disciples once more. But before Jesus returns to heaven, He tells His friends, "I will ask the Father, and he will give you another Counselor to be with you forever. He is the Spirit of truth. The world is unable to receive him because it doesn't see him or know him. But you do know him, because he remains with you and will be in you" (John 14:16–17). Jesus does not leave us alone on earth but asks God the Father to send the Holy Spirit to live inside those who love Him.

Because, as followers of Jesus, we have the Spirit within us, we can pray with the power of the Spirit. The Holy Spirit knows every inch of our souls and understands the things we need and want even more than we understand ourselves. There are times we feel so sad, angry, or joyful that we do not have the words to say. In those moments, we have the Holy Spirit inside of us, praying on our behalf (Romans 8:26–27). Other times, we might feel too small and insignificant to ask God for anything, but then, too, we have the gift of the Spirit to give us power and boldness in prayer.

When believers pray, their prayers are not just said by themselves alone but also by the Spirit inside them. God is praying with us, and His power is available to us when we pray in His will. We can trust God to hear us and know us because the Spirit is with us always, praying on our behalf. Let us seek His guidance in our lives.

We can trust God to hear us and know us because the Spirit is with us always.

WE CAN PRESENT OUR
REQUESTS TO GOD AND
trust Him to act
IN HIS OWN PERFECT
TIMING AND WAYS.

REFLECT REFLECT REFLECT

What is something new you learned about God today?

_____

_____

_____

_____

How does praying in the Spirit change
the way you view prayer?

_____

_____

_____

_____

Write a prayer to God below. You can praise Him, thank
Him, cry out to Him, or ask for something from Him (or
all of the above!). Pray this prayer with the Spirit, trusting
that God is praying this with you if you believe in Him.

_____

_____

_____

_____

_____

_____

_____

_____

_____

_____

_____

WHEN WE PRAY
GOD'S WORD,
WE ARE PRAYING
FOR THINGS
God cares about.

SPIRITUAL DISCIPLINE

PRAYING SCRIPTURE

God gave us His Word to guide us. This guidance includes prayer. Jesus gave us a template for how to pray in the book of Matthew (Matthew 6:9–13), and we can read the prayers of many other characters in the Bible, as well.

One of the most prayerful people in the Bible was a king named David. He was known as a man after God's own heart because he cried out to God in praise, anger, sadness, confusion, and every other emotion under the sun. We can look to the prayers recorded in God's Word to learn how to pray, and we can even pray portions of Scripture back to God.

YOU CAN PRAY SCRIPTURE WHEN:

1. **You do not have the words to pray.** Sometimes there are difficult circumstances or feelings you want help with, but you do not know what to say. You can use God's Word as prayer when your own heart does not have the words.

2. **You do not know what to pray for.** Sometimes you can get stuck praying for the same things over and over, or sometimes you just may not be sure what you should pray for. When we pray God's Word, we are praying for things God cares about. You are part of growing God's kingdom when you pray for the things God wants for this world.

PRACTICE:

Read Psalm 119:33–40 carefully. Do your best to understand the heart behind this passage. Then, pray the words of God back to God so that your heart might be changed to be more like His.

WEEK FOUR WEEK FOUR WEEK FOUR WEEK FOUR WEEK FOUR WEEK FOUR WEEK FOUR WEEK FOUR WEEK FOUR WEEK FOUR WEEK FOUR WEEK FOUR WEEK FOUR

THE STORY OF JESUS

HE IS BORN!

Think of your favorite Christmas tradition, if you have one. Christmas is typically a season of joy and excitement as we look forward to eating cookies, singing songs about snowmen, and opening presents. The anticipation we feel as Christmas draws closer each year reflects the eager waiting of God's people before the birth of Jesus.

Ever since the first sin of Adam and Eve, the world has been broken. Every one of us chooses sin rather than obedience to God; consequently, we are spiritually dead and distanced from Him. But God promised His people throughout the Old Testament that a Savior was coming to mend the brokenness, and so they waited. They waited for generations and generations as leaders rose and fell, but still, their hearts longed for the one true Savior, the Messiah.

Two of Israel's leaders during this time of waiting were David and Solomon. King David was strong, faithful, and handsome but committed adultery and murder. His son Solomon was rich and wise but grew greedy and amassed hundreds of wives. Each time a new great leader arose in Israel, the people's hope increased, wondering if, this time, their Messiah might be here. Yet each time, that person failed. Then, Israel sat in silence and hoped that help was on the way for four hundred years. They waited and waited until one night when a star shone brightly, piercing through the darkness.

Matthew 1:18 picks up at this point in God's story of redemption. As we read, we are introduced to Mary and Joseph, who are betrothed. To be "betrothed" might sound like a foreign concept to us, but if we were to compare it to today's cultural standards, it would be somewhere between being engaged and being married. Mary and Joseph did not yet live together, but they were more committed than we would typically think about an engaged couple. At this point in their relationship, the only way to end their betrothal would be to divorce. During this time, Mary becomes pregnant even though she is a virgin (Matthew 1:18). Joseph, believing Mary must have been unfaithful to him, decides to divorce her quietly and move on with his life. That is, until an angel from God reveals God's plan. Joseph obeys, and together, Mary and Joseph welcome a baby into the world.

This wasn't just any baby—this baby would finally fulfill all of God's promises, starting with Mary. Hundreds of years before Mary was even born, God offered a glimpse of Jesus's birth when He promised a prophet named Isaiah that a virgin would give birth. Isaiah wrote a promise down in Isaiah 7:14 that says, "Therefore, the Lord himself will give you a sign: See, the virgin will conceive, have a son, and name him Immanuel." God revealed His plan hundreds of years before it happened. The virgin birth of Jesus was a sign that the Savior of the world was finally here.

The prophet Isaiah foretold even more about this Savior in Isaiah 9:6, which says, "For a child will be born for us, a son will be given to us, and the government will be on his shoulders. He will be named Wonderful Counselor, Mighty God, Eternal Father, Prince of Peace." The birth of Jesus means the birth of Someone wiser than Solomon and more powerful than David—Someone who would live forever and bring peace to the world. In Jesus, Someone new and unique is born. Never before had a virgin given birth or had God come to dwell among us. The word "dwell" in John 1:14 is the Greek word *skenoō*, which means "pitched his tent." God the Son left heaven to live among us and become our neighbor. We chose a life separated from God due to sin, but He chose to draw close to us. Jesus wants to be near us and know us so much that He became flesh and walked the earth as one of us. Then, he died and returned to life to end the separation between Him and us forever.

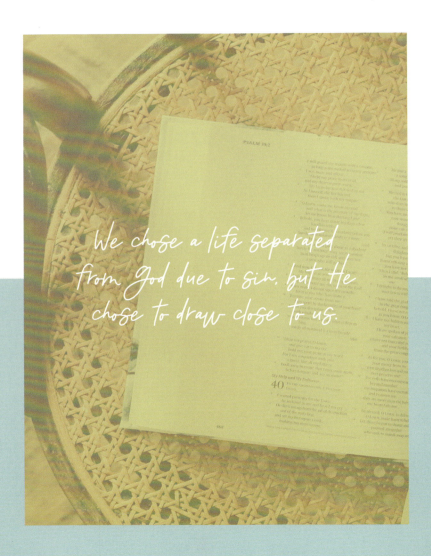

We chose a life separated from God due to sin, but He chose to draw close to us.

REFLECT REFLECT REFLECT REFLECT

How do we know that Jesus was the promised Savior?

_____

_____

_____

_____

_____

What does Jesus do to be close to us?

_____

_____

_____

_____

_____

Why does God want to dwell with us?
(Look at Genesis 1:27, John 3:16, and Ephesians 2:10.)

_____

_____

_____

_____

_____

_____

_____

_____

_____

_____

_____

AS YOU READ THE OLD TESTAMENT, LOOK FOR SIGNS THAT POINT TO *the coming of Jesus.*

JESUS IN

THE OLD TESTAMENT

Jesus is not absent from the Old Testament. John 1:1–2 says, "In the beginning was the Word, and the Word was with God, and the Word was God. He was with God in the beginning." In these verses, Jesus is identified as "the Word." As we discussed on Week 3 Day 5, Jesus is God the Son and thus a part of the Trinity, which means He has always been and always will be. God the Son was there in the beginning when the first light splashed the earth with color. He took part in the creation of each star and planet in the sky. We can see glimpses of Him throughout the Old Testament as generations awaited His arrival.

The whole of Scripture points to God and His plan to save us through His Son. One example of how Scripture points to God's plan is in Luke 24:44, when Jesus says, "These are my words that I spoke to you while I was still with you—that everything written about me in the Law of Moses, the Prophets, and the Psalms must be fulfilled." Jesus fulfills all the requirements of the Old Testament Law and Messianic prophecies, which are God's promises about the Savior. As you read the Old Testament, look for signs that point to the coming of Jesus.

The whole of Scripture points to God and His plan to save us through His Son.

These are just a few of many examples of Jesus in the Old Testament. Look up each Scripture to see how the promises of God in the Old Testament are fulfilled in Jesus.

Old Testament Promise	New Testament Fulfillment	What It Means
Genesis 3:15	1 Corinthians 15:54–57	Jesus crushed the head of Satan by conquering sin and death on the cross.
Genesis 12:3	Matthew 1:1	Jesus came from the line of Abraham and blessed all nations through His death on the cross.
Genesis 49:10	Matthew 1:2	Jesus came from the line of Judah and rules as King. A scepter (mentioned in Genesis 49:10) is a staff held by kings.
2 Samuel 7:12–16; Jeremiah 23:5	Matthew 1:1	Jesus was from the family line of David and now sits on an eternal throne.
Psalm 118:22	Ephesians 2:19–20	Jesus was rejected by this world but became the cornerstone for salvation.

Old Testament Promise	New Testament Fulfillment	What It Means
Isaiah 7:14	Matthew 1:22–23	Jesus was born to a virgin mother, Mary.
Isaiah 11:1	Matthew 1:5–6	Jesus was from the family line of Jesse.
Micah 5:2	Matthew 2:1	Jesus was born in Bethlehem.
Isaiah 40:3–5; Malachi 3:1	Luke 3:4–6	John the Baptist prepared the way for Jesus's ministry.
Zechariah 12:10	John 19:37	Jesus was pierced on His side while on the cross.
Isaiah 53:6–12	Luke 23:32; John 19:38–42; Romans 4:25	Jesus suffered for the sins of the world, died between two thieves, and was buried in a rich man's tomb.

COME AND SEE

READ JOHN 1:35–51

Have you ever attended a concert? There is a sense of anticipation before each one begins. Some fans arrive hours in advance just to be sure they have a spot close to the stage, while others talk with friends about their excitement to see a performance for weeks. Even when the show starts, the anticipation lingers throughout the opening act. Though it might be a great band or singer, it is not who you came to see.

We can think of John the Baptist as the opening act. He was sent by God to announce the coming of the Savior, the One we have been waiting for ever since the fall of Adam and Eve. When John sees Jesus, he is ready to perform his job and let the world know who has finally arrived. The opening act is now over, and it is time to announce the main event.

John refers to Jesus as "the Lamb of God." This phrase comes from Isaiah 53:7, which says, "He was oppressed and afflicted, yet he did not open his mouth. Like a lamb led to the slaughter and like a sheep silent before her shearers, he did not open his mouth." Just like a sheep silently offers its wool so that others can be warm, Jesus will sacrifice Himself so that we can be freed from the punishment of sin.

However, some people in this story seem to be confused by Jesus's identity. Nathanael is one of them. When told about a man named Jesus from a town called Nazareth, Nathanael asks, "Can anything good come out of Nazareth?" (verse 46). Then, when he meets Jesus, he expresses further confusion, asking Jesus, "How do you know me?" (verse 48). Maybe you have felt equally confused about who Jesus is as you sit in church or around the dinner table. People might talk to you about Jesus, but you do not understand what it all means. You might wonder how Jesus would respond to your questions about Him. Thankfully, we know from studying Scripture exactly how He would respond.

When confronted by these men's curiosity, Jesus simply tells them, "Come and you'll see" (John 1:39). He offers for them to watch how He acts and listen to what He says. He does not tell them they need to be good or work hard to earn the right to get to know Him. These men spend three years as friends and followers of Jesus. They eat, laugh, cry, and work with Him. They watch Him miraculously heal the blind, feed the five thousand, and walk on water. And it all started with one word—"Come."

The men in this story all end up as disciples of Jesus, but they arrive there in different ways. Some follow because of what others say about Jesus, some because of what they hear Jesus say for themselves, and others follow because their friends or family members tell them to follow Jesus. No matter their path, Jesus offers each of them a relationship with Him because He loves them. He is the Lamb of God who sacrifices Himself for the sins of the world. That is Someone worth getting to know.

There are many ways God calls us to Himself, but He often uses His people and His Word. Maybe this guide was given to you, or perhaps you found it on your own. Either way, if you find yourself wanting to know more about Jesus, it is because He is calling you to Himself. He knows everything about you, and He desires for you to know Him, too. You do not need to work hard or complete a list of good deeds in order to get to know Jesus. He wants to start a relationship with you exactly as you are right now. If you already have a relationship with Him, you can invite your family and friends to get to know Him. You do not need to have all the answers. Instead, you can invite them to come and see for themselves.

IF YOU FIND YOURSELF
WANTING TO KNOW
MORE ABOUT JESUS,
IT IS BECAUSE
He is calling you
TO HIMSELF.

REFLECT REFLECT REFLECT

What qualifications do you think Jesus would have for His
followers? (e.g., should they be really smart or strong?)

_____

_____

_____

_____

_____

The men Jesus chose as His disciples were not
who we would typically expect. For example, several
of them were fishermen, and Scripture calls them
"uneducated and untrained men" (Acts 4:13).
Why do you think Jesus called them to be His disciples?

_____

_____

_____

_____

What does it mean to follow Jesus?

_____

_____

_____

_____

_____

_____

_____

_____

_____

MIRACLES

READ MARK 4:35–41; LUKE 7:11–17

We are amazed by talented people. We want to watch games with the best players, shows with incredible singers, and videos of people attempting the impossible. These talented people are known for what they do but not always for who they are. Jesus does and says amazing things throughout His life that no one expects. Many of these acts are called miracles. A miracle is an act of God that occurs supernaturally, which means it could not have happened naturally in the world. Miracles are actions that no one else but God would ever be able to do, and they are fascinating. That is why we often see huge crowds following Jesus around. They want to see what He will do and say next because it is astounding. However, unlike athletes or performers who show their talents to gain their own glory and fame, Jesus performs these miracles to glorify God.

Jesus does not perform miracles to get famous or powerful. In fact, He often commands the people He heals to stay silent about it. Instead, these miracles serve as signs that Jesus really is the Son of God so that we can have faith in what He says and does on the cross. Jesus reveals His power over creation, the enemy, and disease to show that He has the power to free us from the stronghold of sin and death.

In Mark 4:35–41, Jesus's disciples are terrified by the giant waves that are about to destroy their boat. They run to Jesus and ask if

He even cares about them anymore. With a word, Jesus immediately stops the wind and the waves, just as God created them with a word in Genesis. The disciples see the power of God in Jesus through this miracle.

Jesus also performs miracles out of love. He has compassion on the hurting and suffering. In Luke 7:11–17, the mother of the dead man has found herself alone in the world. Her husband has died, and now her only son is gone too, which puts her in a vulnerable situation. In this culture, a woman needed the financial support of either a husband or a male child, or she would become a beggar. The moment her son dies, she faces burying her only family member and facing destitution all at once. Jesus sees this woman in her need and comes near to heal, raising her son to life. Through this act of love, the crowds following Jesus see His power over death and glorify God because of it.

However, the greatest miracle of all is Jesus's death on the cross and His resurrection three days later. Out of great love for us, Jesus sacrificed Himself to heal the wounds of our sins and show us the power of God. Jesus is not just a miracle worker or gifted teacher. He is the Son of God who came to save the world from sin. His teachings and miracles all reflect the power of God and are meant to guide us back into a relationship with Him. Let us look not only at the works of Jesus but also at the power and purpose behind them.

Jesus is not just a miracle worker or gifted teacher. He is the Son of God.

THE GREATEST MIRACLE
OF ALL IS JESUS'S DEATH
ON THE CROSS AND
His resurrection
THREE DAYS LATER.

Make a list below of all the miracles of Jesus you can remember. Flip through the Gospels (Matthew, Mark, Luke, and John) if you cannot think of any.

_____

_____

_____

_____

_____

_____

_____

Why does Jesus perform miracles?

_____

_____

_____

_____

_____

_____

_____

How do miracles help us trust in Jesus's words?

_____

_____

_____

_____

_____

_____

_____

THE CROSS

Before a word is spoken, Jesus knows why these men are there. He understands the trial He will face, the humiliation and pain He will endure, and the ultimate death He will experience, all before it happens. Jesus is God and has known about this plan since the beginning. He tells His disciples that He will have to die, but they fail to understand. But even though Jesus knows exactly what will happen, He still chooses to go. He does not run or try to talk His way out of the situation. When Peter tries to defend Jesus, Jesus commands him to stop. When leaders question Jesus, He does not try to defend Himself but instead asks questions back to show these men their own faulty thinking, or He remains silent. Jesus is not a victim but a willing participant. He chooses to die in this way because it is the only path for us to experience true life. This is why He came.

Many Jews expected the promised Messiah to be a military conqueror. They thought He would liberate them from the oppressive rule of Rome and restore the kingdom of Israel. However, Jesus's battle was not against a government but against sin. He did not need a sword but a wooden cross. Jesus did not shed the blood of His enemies but instead allowed His own to be shed for His enemies. It is difficult to live in this world, and sometimes our struggles are not against other humans. Paul, the author of the book of Ephesians, explains this in Ephesians 6:12, which says, "For our struggle is not against flesh and blood, but against the rulers, against the authorities, against the cosmic powers of this darkness, against evil, spiritual forces in the heavens." This is the ultimate battle we all fight. It is not a physical war but a spiritual one. We face temptation and darkness daily, but we are not alone in that battle. Jesus died for us, and God sent the Holy Spirit to be with us so that we do not fight on our own. The story of the cross is not a story of defeat because Jesus completed His rescue mission. We are now free from the punishment of death when we place our faith in the One who gave up everything for us.

As Jesus faced death on a cross, He was betrayed by everyone close to Him. One of His disciples, Judas, turned Him over to the Jewish authorities for a few pieces of silver; these leaders put Him on trial without cause; and one of His best friends, Peter, denied knowing Him three times in a row. We, too, betray Jesus. We choose sin over Him every day. Though a convicted criminal, Barabbas, should have been crucified, his life is exchanged for the innocent life of Jesus. We, too, are like Barabbas. We are sinners who deserve punishment for our sin, but Jesus trades His life for ours on the cross.

As He takes His last breaths on the cross, Jesus says, "It is finished" (John 19:30). After the guards ensure Jesus is really dead, His body is taken and buried in a tomb. His disciples are left believing this is the end, and they all scatter in fear of meeting the same fate as their leader. But this is not the end—because Jesus is coming back.

Jesus did not shed the blood of His enemies but instead allowed His own to be shed for His enemies.

THE STORY OF THE CROSS
IS NOT A STORY OF
DEFEAT BECAUSE JESUS
COMPLETED
His rescue mission.

REFLECT REFLECT REFLECT

Why does it matter that Jesus was a
willing participant and not a victim?

_____
_____
_____
_____

Look at the cross below. Take a moment to write down
anything you say or do that betrays Jesus. Reflect on the
fact that Jesus paid for those sins on your behalf.

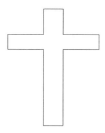

Write a prayer, thanking Jesus for His work on
the cross. Think about how freedom from
the punishment of sin changes your life.

_____
_____
_____
_____
_____
_____
_____
_____

THE RESURRECTION

READ JOHN 20; ROMANS 6:4

Three days after watching His death, Mary Magdalene visits Jesus's tomb in order to finish preparing His body for burial. She followed Jesus faithfully all the way to the cross and now shows her respect and love for Jesus by completing the rituals for death. To her dismay, she finds the tomb empty. Her teacher and leader is gone, and she guesses that His body has been taken somewhere else. She is hurt, alone, and crying until a man arrives. Mary does not know who this man is until He says her name. At that moment, Mary realizes that the man she is crying over is standing right in front of her.

The man who greets Mary, then the disciples, and finally Thomas, is, without a doubt, Jesus. He knows Mary's name, and the scars from the nails that pierced His hands as He hung on the cross are visible. No one snatched His body away because the cloth that was placed over His face after death is carefully folded inside of the tomb, and no grave robber would take the time to tidy up. Thomas at first doubts Jesus's resurrection from the dead, perhaps believing the disciples saw a ghost or a figment of their imagination. But then, Jesus stands before him. Thomas can touch His hands and know that Jesus is truly alive again.

Even though Jesus told His followers time and time again that He would die but come back, they never understood what He meant. Mary does not see Jesus for who He truly is until He says her name, and the disciples do not believe until Jesus stands before them. Like-wise, many people sit in churches around the world today and do not understand who Jesus is. They know the facts of Jesus but not the person. In His own time, Jesus reveals Himself to Mary, the dis-ciples, and Thomas. After appearing to His disciples and spending time with them, Jesus returns to heaven (Acts 1:9), but He does not leave His followers alone. He sends the Holy Spirit (Acts 2), the third member of the Trinity, to help His disciples realize the meaning of His teachings and understand that the Old Testament and Jesus Himself foretold the cross and resurrection. The disciples could not understand all of this without God's help, and neither can we. We need God's help. Thankfully, when we put our faith in Jesus, He also imparts the Holy Spirit to us (Romans 8:9). Jesus does not leave us to figure it all out on our own, but instead, the Holy Spirit enlightens our hearts and minds to the truth of the gospel.

Now that Jesus is alive again, there is an open door to His family. When we believe that He is the Son of God who chose to die on the cross for our sins, we become not just followers but brothers and sisters of Jesus. As members of this family, our old lives are buried in the ground just as Jesus was. When we accept Him as our Sav-ior, we are given new hearts and raised to new life in Him. We are not who we once were and do not have to live with the guilt of sin because Jesus covers our sin with His blood. Instead, we can live in freedom from shame and walk in joyful obedience to God because of our love for Him.

The Holy Spirit enlightens our hearts and minds to the truth of the gospel.

WE CAN PRESENT OUR
REQUESTS TO GOD AND
trust Him to act
IN HIS OWN PERFECT
TIMING AND WAYS.

Read 1 Corinthians 15:17 and Philippians 1:21
to answer the questions below.

What does "to live is Christ" mean?

_____

_____

_____

_____

_____

_____

What do we gain from death?

_____

_____

_____

_____

_____

Why did Jesus need to come back to life?
(Hint: look at 1 Corinthians.)

_____

_____

_____

_____

_____

_____

WRITING HIS STORY

In Week 1, we spent a whole day covering the gospel. Feel free to go back and look at Week 1 Day 4 as a reminder. The gospel is the heart of Christianity. The word "gospel" comes from a Greek term, *euangelion*, which means "good news." In Ancient Greece, *euangelion* was used to announce good news ranging from a victorious battle to a new emperor taking the throne.

Followers of Jesus should know the gospel for the formation of their own faith but also to announce this good news to the entire world. Just after Jesus rose from the dead, He met with His disciples and told them, "All authority has been given to me in heaven and on earth. Go, therefore, and make disciples of all nations, baptizing them in the name of the Father and of the Son and of the Holy Spirit, teaching them to observe everything I have commanded you. And remember, I am with you always, to the end of the age" (Matthew 28:18–20). This command, now called "The Great Commission," is true for everyone who has faith in Jesus. We get to share the amazing news of the gospel with others so that they can share in the joy we have in Jesus.

Today, you will practice sharing the gospel with someone else. In the lines below, write down how you would share the gospel with a friend. Then, practice saying it aloud a few times until it feels comfortable. Finally, if there is someone in your life who needs to hear this good news, pray for courage, and share the gospel with them in your own words.

What is the gospel? Think about the problem of sin and the solution of the cross in your answer.

_____

_____

_____

_____

_____

_____

_____

_____

The gospel is the heart of Christianity.

WEEK FIVE WEEK FIVE WEEK FIVE WEEK FIVE WEEK FIVE WEEK FIVE WEEK FIVE WEEK FIVE WEEK FIVE

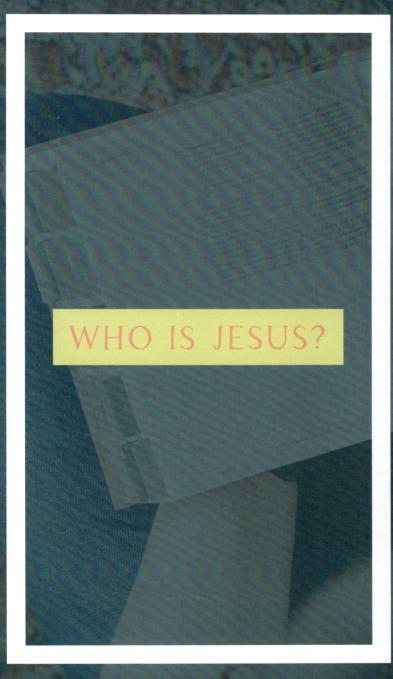

WHO IS JESUS?

JESUS IS COMPASSIONATE

READ MARK 5:21–43

A religious leader named Jairus comes up to Jesus in the middle of a huge crowd begging Him to heal his daughter. Even though Jairus is powerful and respected, he humbles himself in front of Jesus by falling to Jesus's feet and begging Him to heal. You might expect Jesus to ignore the pleas of this leader. However, Jesus is not like everyone else. When He hears the hurt of this father, He turns to help. Pushing through the crowd, Jesus moves to heal not only the pain of the daughter but also the hurt of this father who does not want to lose his child.

As Jesus walks through the crowd, a woman comes up to Him in desperation. For twelve years, she has suffered with no relief. All her money is gone, spent on doctors who could not fix her. In fact, her condition only worsened. Not only is this bleeding likely painful physically, but it also keeps this woman unclean according to Old Testament law (Leviticus 15:25–27). She cannot sit on a piece of furniture or touch another person without making them unclean. Because of this, we can imagine that no one wants to be around this woman, so she likely lives in isolation and embarrassment along with pain for over a decade. But then, she sees Jesus and perhaps comes to realize that this is the only option for healing she has not tried. She reaches for His clothes, and immediately, Jesus turns and looks at this hurting woman with love and compassion. He is not angry that she draws near or frustrated that she stops Him in the middle of His journey to heal someone else. Jesus is never too busy to help those who need Him. Instead, He stops to comfort and heal her. This woman is not powerful, rich, or respected like Jairus, but that does not matter to Jesus. Jesus's desire is to heal anyone who asks and believes.

However, in the time it takes to stop and speak with the bleeding woman, Jairus receives a devastating piece of news. Jesus is too late. His daughter has died. We can imagine that all of Jairus's hope died, too, in that moment. After all, who has power over death? Yet Jesus continues on to see this now-dead girl. He leaves the crowd and focuses only on the pain of this one family. He is not interested in fame or the spotlight but instead cares for those who are hurting. When Jesus speaks, this girl immediately comes back from the dead. In one moment, Jesus heals the girl's disease as well as the grief of her family.

Jesus heals the rich and powerful alongside the poor and outcast. Your appearance, education, age, and social status do not change the way He sees you. Jesus loves when those who need help come to Him, for He is the only One able to fully heal us. He died on the cross and rose to free us from the pain of sin and death. Come to Him with your hurts, struggles, and pain, and trust that He cares about them as deeply as He cared about Jairus, his daughter, and the bleeding woman.

Jesus is never too busy to help those who need Him.

Jesus's desire
IS TO HEAL ANYONE
WHO ASKS AND BELIEVES.

REFLECT REFLECT REFLECT REFLECT

Have you ever felt that God was too busy for you?
If so, what does this passage teach instead?

_____

_____

_____

_____

_____

Do you pray to Jesus when you are hurting?
Why or why not?

_____

_____

_____

_____

_____

Write a prayer, asking God to bring healing
wherever it is needed in your life.

_____

_____

_____

_____

_____

_____

_____

_____

_____

JESUS IS SYMPATHETIC

READ LUKE 4:1–13; HEBREWS 4:14–16

Have you ever tried to comfort someone but felt like you did not know what to say because you have never gone through what they are going through? It is difficult to help someone when you have not experienced the same situation as them. In a similar way, some assume that God is distant from us and our problems or that He cannot understand the complexities of our lives all the way in heaven. However, because Jesus left heaven to live on earth, He understands what it is to be human.

In today's reading, we see that Jesus is fully man. He feels hungry, tired, and thirsty. Jesus has just been baptized and then goes into the wilderness to fast after being prompted by the Holy Spirit. When He is on the brink of starvation after not eating for forty days, the enemy appears. This enemy goes by many names, including "the tempter." This is the enemy that disguised himself as a snake and led Adam and Eve into the first sin (Genesis 3). He now appears to Jesus when He is physically weak. The tempter often shows up when we are the most vulnerable. He lies and manipulates in order to draw God's creation away from Him. For example, when we feel tired or guilty about not studying, we can find ourselves tempted to cheat on a test. When we feel unworthy or lonely, we can feel tempted to do anything necessary to fit in or end the pain. We often give in to these temptations, especially in our moments of weakness, leading us to sin.

We read that Jesus is tempted in three ways. First, He is tempted to satisfy His own needs rather than trusting God to do so. He is hungry, so the tempter tells Him to use His power to turn a stone into bread even though He is choosing to fast, or go without food. We are often tempted to satisfy ourselves rather than trust that God will give us what we need in His timing. Jesus, though, chooses to wait on His Father.

Second, the tempter offers Jesus fame, fortune, and comfort. The tempter tells Jesus that He can rule over the entire world but only if He bows down to the enemy. We often feel this temptation. We want all that this world has to offer, and we are willing to do whatever it takes to get what we want. Jesus, however, knows that only God is worthy of worship, and so He again refuses to sin.

Third, the tempter commands Jesus to throw Himself off of a giant building to see if God will protect Him. Often we attempt to test God like this. We promise to obey Him if He proves to us He is real by getting school canceled or helping us pass a test. But Jesus knows that God is the One in control, and it is not right to test Him. While the rest of us bow to temptation, Jesus remains firm in faithfulness to God.

Because Jesus never allows temptation to lead to sin, He can offer us freedom from the punishment for our sin. When we do allow temptation to control us, Jesus does not shame us for it. Instead, Jesus offers mercy and understanding because He has gone through the pain of temptation Himself. We can confess to Jesus because He forgives, and we can seek His comfort because He knows exactly what we are going through.

While the rest of us bow to temptation, Jesus remains firm in faithfulness to God.

Jesus offers mercy AND UNDERSTANDING BECAUSE HE HAS GONE THROUGH THE PAIN OF TEMPTATION HIMSELF.

REFLECT REFLECT REFLECT

Why does it matter that Jesus was tempted just like us?

_____

_____

_____

_____

_____

What is something you are often tempted to do?

_____

_____

_____

_____

_____

Pray that the Holy Spirit will help you
fight that temptation today.

_____

_____

_____

_____

_____

_____

_____

_____

_____

_____

_____

JESUS IS GENEROUS

READ MATTHEW 14:13–21

We learn at a young age that you have to pay for what you want. If you want to go out with friends, you have to finish the chores. If you want someone's chocolate chip cookie at lunch, you have to trade them something good for it. If you want good presents under the Christmas tree, you make sure to act nice to your siblings. Our world runs on working for what you want. But when Jesus comes to this world, He offers a new way to live.

In today's passage, Jesus hears that His cousin, John the Baptist, has been murdered, and He goes off to be alone. However, the people around Jesus are so desperate to hear and see Him that they follow Him. Most people would be frustrated to have someone bother them as they are trying to be alone, but not Jesus. He sees this crowd that is hungry for leadership and guidance, and He has compassion on them. Even though He seeks solitude, Jesus goes to the crowd to teach and heal. After a full day of this, everyone is tired and hungry. The people need food and rest. The disciples realize this and tell Jesus that He should release the crowd to go get what they need in town. Jesus, however, has a grander plan.

Seeing the crowd's hunger, Jesus wants to give the people what they need—Himself. Armed with only two fish and five small loaves of bread, Jesus plans to feed thousands. This is like trying to feed an entire high school with a peanut butter and jelly sandwich and a bag of chips. If you split this small meal among thousands, all anyone will get are tiny crumbs. And yet, when Jesus breaks the bread, everyone eats until they are fully satisfied. Not only is there enough for everyone to eat until they are full, but there are even leftovers. Jesus performs a miracle to provide generously to others.

This crowd needed food, and Jesus provided it. What about you? What do you need? Do you try to meet your needs yourself, or do you turn to Jesus? Matthew 6:25–34 reminds us that we don't have to be anxious about our daily needs because Jesus will provide for our every need. With the hungry crowd gathered around, Jesus could have given each person a small snack to tide them over until they got home. But instead, He chose to give them a feast where they had all they needed to eat and more. In doing so, He proves His generosity and capability to provide for His children.

Jesus is more generous than anyone the world has ever known. His greatest act of generosity is giving up His life for ours on the cross. When we are lacking in life, Jesus is the answer. He does not provide for us because of our good works, eloquent prayers, or even because we ask. He gives out of an overflow of love for us. Life in God's kingdom does not require us to work for what we want. Instead, this upside-down kingdom offers us a King who works on our behalf to provide us what we need while His subjects sit and receive the blessing of His work. Then, we can do good works out of love for God rather than out of a need to get something from Him. We do not need to search this world to fill our lives. Instead, we can sit at the feet of Jesus and trust He will provide for us because of His love and generosity.

Jesus is more generous than anyone the world has ever known.

WHEN JESUS COMES TO
THIS WORLD, HE OFFERS
a new way to live.

REFLECT REFLECT REFLECT REFLECT

What has God given to you out of His generosity?
Consider talents, relationships, or parts
of His creation that you enjoy.

_____
_____
_____
_____
_____
_____
_____
_____

How does this story change the way you pray?

_____
_____
_____
_____
_____
_____
_____

Where can you show generosity like Jesus?

_____
_____
_____
_____
_____
_____
_____

JESUS IS POWERFUL

READ MARK 5:1–20; JOHN 14:12

What is power? Most of us want it, but we all define it differently. For some, power is strength. For others, it is money or success in business or politics. It could be intelligence. No matter how you define it, we all want power of some sort. We want power over our own lives, power over what our government does, or power in our friend groups. In today's reading, Jesus meets a man who is incredibly powerful but only because he is consumed by a spirit that overpowers his life.

Jesus meets a demoniac, or a person who is harassed, oppressed, or possessed by an evil spirit. The demoniac's entire life is in shambles because he has lost control to a legion of demons. He lives alone, surrounded by the dead in a graveyard. Others tried to help this man by placing him in shackles so that he could not hurt himself or others, but they were powerless against this oppression. Others are scared of this man, and he lives in misery.

One day, Jesus appears. The spirit inside of this man instantly recognizes Jesus as the Son of God and begs for His mercy. The spirit that inspired such fear and sadness now stands afraid of someone infinitely more powerful. The legion knows that Jesus has complete control over it and does not even try to fight Him. Instead, it immediately leaves the man who is now free from oppression. This man, unlike the evil spirit, begs to remain close to Jesus, but Jesus commands him to go out and tell his own people of Jesus's power and love.

Jesus is more powerful than any physical or spiritual being. There is nothing in the universe stronger, wiser, or wealthier than Him. Jesus frees people from disease, demons, and even death. We often feel overpowered by the darkness in this world. There are people we fear, habits that seem to control us, and circumstances that overwhelm us. We are consumed by guilt, anger, lust, greed, and jealousy, and there are days when we believe we will never be free of these forces in our lives. But none of this is too big or scary for Jesus. An entire legion of demons shakes in their boots at the mere sight of Him. Death itself is conquered by Jesus on the cross. We can bring our fears to Jesus and trust that He is powerful enough to end them. He comes to those who are hurting and brings healing. Jesus uses His power to offer us freedom.

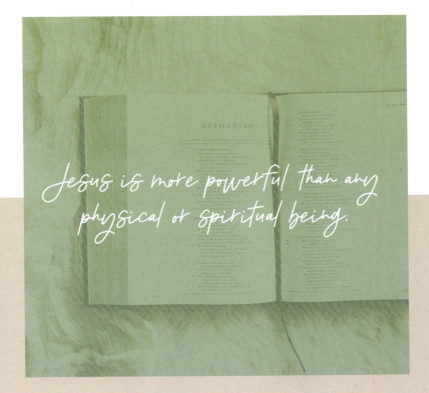

Jesus is more powerful than any physical or spiritual being.

JESUS USES HIS
POWER TO OFFER US
freedom.

REFLECT REFLECT REFLECT

What is something that controls your
life right now, other than God?

_____

_____

_____

_____

_____

Fill in the blank with your answer from #1, and then say
this sentence out loud three times: *Jesus is stronger than...*

_____

_____

_____

_____

_____

What does Jesus ask the demoniac to do once he is free?
What can we learn from this?

_____

_____

_____

_____

_____

_____

_____

_____

_____

_____

_____

JESUS IS MERCIFUL

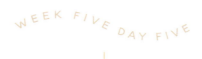

READ LUKE 15:11–24

Imagine a time when you knew you messed up and your parents found out. Perhaps fear rises up from your stomach and into your throat until you have trouble swallowing. Realizing you are in trouble, you prepare to beg your parents for mercy. In your head, you think of all the things you will say or promise to do to get rid of their anger. But then, they walk up to you, smile, and give you a hug. Relief floods over your body, as well as confusion, because you know you deserve their wrath, yet you receive immediate forgiveness.

Jesus tells us a story in the book of Luke about a son who makes many mistakes. First, he essentially tells his dad he wishes him dead so that he can take his share of his dad's money to live on his own. The dad, letting his son choose, allows him to take the money and go. The son abandons his family to live on his own terms. But this does not go well. After wasting all of the money on good times, the son is poor and alone.

At his lowest point, the son finally remembers he has a dad with great wealth. As the son walks home, he likely starts to think of all the ways he is going to beg for forgiveness. In this time period, a father was considered the authoritative leader of his home. His word was final, and his honor was to be maintained by everyone in his family.

The son realizes the shame he brought to his father the day he left, and he recognizes his inability to restore the honor his family lost. He expects to live as a servant in his own family's home. He probably pictures his father yelling or punishing him for his choices, and he knows that is what he deserves. But, in reality, the father has been waiting for his son to come back ever since he left—not to shame him or yell at him but because he loves him and wants to be near him. When the dad sees his son, he runs as fast as he can and embraces his lost child, who is now found. The dad's desire to welcome his son back home, even after he had done wrong, ultimately demonstrates the dad's great mercy and love for his son.

We are all like the son in the story. We choose to live a life apart from God on our own terms. In other words, we sin. Sin comes from inside our hearts when we decide to love ourselves and the world more than we love our God. Like the son, life on our own tends not to go very well. We feel lonely, angry, purposeless, and overall lacking in what we really want. We realize that we need to be close to God, but we know that we do not deserve it because we have run away from Him time after time. Jesus knows that our sin blocks us from a relationship with our Father. Out of mercy, Jesus accepts the punishment we deserve so that we can run back to God as He runs toward us with arms open wide.

Out of mercy, Jesus accepts the punishment we deserve so that we can run back to God.

But the father told his servants,
"Quick! Bring out the best robe
and put it on him; put a ring on
his finger and sandals on his feet.
Then bring the fattened calf and
slaughter it, and let's celebrate
with a feast, because this son
of mine was dead and is alive
again; he was lost and is found!"
So they began to celebrate.

LUKE 15:22–24

REFLECT REFLECT REFLECT REFLECT

What does the word "mercy" mean?

_____

_____

_____

_____

_____

Take a minute and think about how much Jesus
loves you—so much that He would leave heaven and
come to earth to show you mercy. Do you believe Jesus
loves you that much? Why or why not?

_____

_____

_____

_____

_____

Read Luke 6:36–37. How can you be merciful like Jesus?

_____

_____

_____

_____

_____

_____

_____

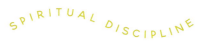

TESTIMONY

Think about a book or movie that changed you. What is your favorite part about it? Most of us love movies and books with incredible stories. Your favorite might have great fight scenes, witty lines, or beautiful scenery, but these features do not generally connect with us on a deep level. Instead, it is a powerful story that changes us. The Bible contains many facts and truths, but what connects with us most is the story found within it: a story of a loving God, a broken people, and a Savior who comes to bring them back together. If you know anything about the Bible, it is probably the stories you remember more than anything else — David and Goliath, Jesus turning water into wine, and Peter walking on water. Stories stick with us in a way that facts generally do not.

The last spiritual discipline we discussed (see page 112) focused on sharing the gospel as fact. This week, the focus will be on sharing the gospel through the lens of your own story. Many call this giving a testimony. Before we talk about what a testimony is, let us determine all the things a testimony is not.

A TESTIMONY IS *NOT*:

1. A way to brag about yourself and your own accomplishments.
2. A story that has to be dramatic and filled with the darkest parts of humanity in order to be important.
3. A story about an imperfect person who meets Jesus and then never has anymore problems.

A TESTIMONY *IS*:

1. The story of who you were before following Jesus, how you came to believe in Him, and what life looks like now.

2. Something that is completely unique to you. Every testimony is different because God created us to be different.

3. A tool that you can use to help others understand what life with Jesus is like.

On the following pages, you can practice writing your testimony as if you were going to share it with a friend. You will want to include the following:

- What life was like before Jesus
- How you came to understand the gospel and believe it is true
- What life looks like now (this can include any struggles you still have)

If you are not following Jesus yet or if you are not sure if you believe, use this space to write out what life looks like right now. How do you want Jesus to change you? What would you like your life to look like? Then, take a moment to pray to God for those things.

The Bible contains many facts and truths, but what connects with us most is the story found within it.

TESTIMONY TESTIMONY

TESTIMONY TESTIMONY

_____

_____

_____

_____

_____

_____

_____

_____

_____

_____

_____

_____

_____

_____

_____

_____

_____

_____

_____

_____

_____

_____

_____

_____

_____

_____

_____

_____

_____

EEK SIX WEEK SIX WEEK S
WEEK SIX WEEK SIX WEEK S
EEK SIX WEEK SIX WEEK S
EEK SIX WEEK SIX WEEK S
EEK SIX WEEK SIX WEEK S
EEK SIX WEEK SIX WEEK S
EEK SIX WEEK SIX WEEK S
EEK SIX WEEK

WHO ARE YOU?

CHILD OF GOD

READ JOHN 1:12–13; ROMANS 8:12–15

So many movies about high school students end at prom. People sometimes talk about that night as the best night of your life, but what happens when the night ends? In a movie, the credits roll, and you move on. In real life, you wake up and do pretty much the same. There is no real difference between your life before and after the prom. Some view the gospel the same way. You confess your faith in Jesus, and then you wake up the next day unsure of what to do next. Is that it?

The Bible tells us that the moment we confess Jesus saved us from our sin, we are new creations (2 Corinthians 5:17). On the outside, our lives might look basically the same, but inside of us, a new heart beats. We were once enemies of God who chose ourselves and this world over His love and kindness. Now, we are children of God, embraced by a Father who runs to us the moment we call. Children of God are chosen by God through adoption. He decides to make us a part of His family and chooses to love us daily just as a good Father would. Every person who confesses that Jesus is God is now a part of this global family.

We now have a Father in heaven to whom we can cry out as a newborn baby cries for her parents. We can go to Him with our desires, hurts, joys, and fears, and He will listen, comfort, and bring peace. God loves His children more deeply than the best dad in the world, and His love for His children never ends. Once you are a part of God's family, you are there forever. There is nothing you can do to lose your status as a child of God (Romans 8:38–39).

We can trust that we are part of God's family if we are led by the Holy Spirit. But what does it mean for the Holy Spirit to lead us? You may wonder how you can be led by someone you cannot even see! Paul provides an answer for us in Romans 8:13–14: "But if by the Spirit you put to death the deeds of the body, you will live. For all those led by God's Spirit are God's sons." The leading of the Spirit is not some mystical idea; it is the power of God's Spirit within us to put to death the desires of our flesh and choose to honor the Lord through our obedience to His Word. Practically, this looks like daily examining our hearts and minds, turning away from our natural sinful inclinations, and turning toward Christ. Ultimately, it is the Holy Spirit who enables us to live in this way and who conforms us, slowly but surely, into the image of His Son (Romans 8:29, 2 Corinthians 3:18).

This does not mean that once a Christian, we will never struggle with sinful desires of the flesh—those temptations will surely remain, for we live in a world broken by sin, and each of us still has a sin nature. However, it does mean that as Christians, the Lord equips us to overcome every temptation and follow His instruction for our lives as we trust and obey Him in every word and deed.

We are adopted as children of God the moment we have faith, and we live as members of that family forever. We can trust that we are His if we walk in the Spirit, choosing to obey His voice and crying out to Him for help.

We are children of God, embraced by a Father who runs to us the moment we call.

GOD LOVES HIS
CHILDREN MORE DEEPLY
THAN THE BEST DAD IN
THE WORLD, AND HIS
LOVE FOR HIS CHILDREN
never ends.

REFLECT REFLECT REFLECT

How do you become a child of God?

_____
_____
_____
_____
_____
_____
_____
_____

What does it mean to you that God is your Father?

_____
_____
_____
_____
_____

Imagine a time when your parents or guardians
were most proud of you. How did that feel?
Now think about God feeling that way about you.
How does that change the way you view God?

_____
_____
_____
_____
_____
_____
_____

COHEIR WITH CHRIST

When you are born into a family, you get access to all that family has. Their house is now your house, and their food is now your food. Many people dream of being born into royalty because of the wealth and power that members of such a family receive. We know that all who believe in Jesus are adopted as children of God. Because we are now in His family, we have access to all His family has.

God is the King of all heaven and earth who rules and reigns forever. At one time, we were all His enemies who chose sin over obedience. But, in His kindness, God rescued us from the enemy, allowing us to enter into His kingdom through the blood of His Son. Any other king would take his enemies and lock them into prisons or use them as slaves. The King of kings, though, not only rescues us but also adopts us as His own. We live with God now and will join Him in heaven when we leave this earth. As God's one and only Son, Jesus is the heir of God, and we look forward to the day when we will dwell with Him as co-heirs in His Kingdom (Romans 8:17). When Jesus died on our behalf, He opened a way for us to be His coheirs in the kingdom. Jesus died not only to free us from death but to bring us into a full and everlasting life.

As heirs with Christ, we receive an inheritance from our Father. God is the ruler of all, so the whole universe is part of our inheritance.

God is eternal, and so our inheritance is as well. No part of what God offers us will ever get old, break, or wear down. This inheritance is life after death, an eternity spent with a loving Father and a community of fellow believers, and a glorified body that will never break down or get old. We receive a forever life with God that is free from pain, sin, death, or disease.

You may think that life on earth should be easy because of your inheritance in Christ. However, just as Jesus's life was not easy, our lives as heirs will include times of suffering. We might encounter opposition from the world or the enemy who wants to strip us of our inheritance. When Jesus encountered opposition, He ran to the Father to pray. He knew He had the power of the King on His side even as He underwent difficulties. Jesus knew that life on earth would be difficult, but He could look forward to the day He was reunited with His Father in glory. We are the sons and daughters of the mighty God. Let us live knowing that the power of God goes before us and that we have eternity to be with Him. We do not live for this world but in expectation of what awaits us when we get to see our Father face to face.

Jesus died not only to free us from death but to bring us into a full and everlasting life.

WE ARE THE SONS AND
DAUGHTERS OF
The mighty god.

REFLECT REFLECT REFLECT REFLECT

What is included in our inheritance from God?

_____

_____

_____

_____

Read Revelation 21:1–22:5. Based on these verses,
draw a picture of what heaven will be like.

How can you live differently knowing that you have eternity
with God ahead of you—not just this present life on earth?

_____

_____

_____

_____

_____

_____

DISCIPLE OF JESUS

READ LUKE 14:26; JOHN 8:31; JOHN 13:34-35

Most of us can think of a teacher, coach, or mentor who we loved. They laughed with us, encouraged us, and opened our eyes to something new. But inevitably, we leave our teachers and coaches behind as we venture into new grades or activities and must start over with someone new.

But there is one teacher, mentor, and coach who will walk beside us throughout our lives and the lives of each of His disciples: Jesus. The word "disciple" comes from the Greek word *matheteuō*, which means "a pupil or one who learns." The first disciples of Jesus followed Him for three years, watching and learning as He taught, healed, and loved those around Him. Every person from then on who follows the teachings of Jesus is also a disciple of Him. As a disciple, we follow Jesus daily. He is the one teacher whose class we will never graduate from. There is always something new to learn about Jesus and different ways to obey Him. Rather than follow Him around the Middle East like the first disciples, we can follow Him by reading His Word and praying.

Jesus and the writers of the New Testament books said many things about how disciples should act, but they all centered around two main commands—love God and others. To follow Jesus means to love Him above anyone else. God made us, saved us, and loves us more than we can imagine. We, in turn, love Him more than anything else in this world. Out of our love for Him, we then go and love others. Our love for God does not diminish our love for our friends and family but actually enhances it. As we learn to love as God loves, we love our friends more sacrificially and our parents more respectfully.

We love God by building our relationship with Him and loving the things He loves. Our friendships deepen as we spend time with and learn about our friends. The same is true of our Savior. Reading and obeying God's Word is a mark of a true disciple of Jesus. Jesus loved others by spending time with them and helping them while He was on earth. Followers of Jesus should do the same as we help the hurting, pray for those in need, and teach others about who Jesus is.

Following Jesus means that our lives will start to mirror His. Jesus's life was not always easy. Many times, He faced persecution and anger from those who did not understand who He was. Ultimately, He was killed by an angry mob who rejected Him and His message. Jesus tells us that we will face the same persecution in this world. In modern western culture, it is unlikely that persecution means we will be killed for our faith in Jesus. However, it might mean that we lose friends, are left out, or get mocked. When you find yourself suffering, remember that the One you follow has felt the same pain and rejection, but He loves you and is with you always. Following Jesus means learning from Him each day and living the same way He did. As we spend time with Him and love those around us, we follow in His footsteps.

To follow Jesus means to love Him above anyone else.

WE LOVE GOD
BY BUILDING
OUR RELATIONSHIP
WITH HIM AND
*loving the things
He loves.*

REFLECT REFLECT REFLECT REFLECT

Read Matthew 28:18–20.
What does Jesus ask all His disciples to do?

_____

_____

_____

_____

Read Matthew 10:21–25. Why can disciples of
Jesus expect suffering in their own lives?

_____

_____

_____

_____

Fill in the body below with ideas about how you can be a
disciple of Jesus with your whole self.

MEMBER OF THE CHURCH

READ ROMANS 12:4–5; 1 CORINTHIANS 12:12–26; COLOSSIANS 1:18

Consider the people you spend the most time with. These are probably your family, close friends, or teammates. Why do you spend time with each of these people? It is because there is something that bonds you together either by blood, interest, or experience. Christ-followers find their eternal family, friends, and teammates in the Church.

We were not made to live alone. Studies on inmates who spent time in solitary confinement show that many prisoners suffer panic attacks, hallucinations, or depression. When God created Adam, He said it was not right for Adam to be alone. After searching and failing to find a suitable partner for him in all of creation, God made another human to work alongside Adam named Eve (Genesis 2:18–23). God created us to live with others. When you become a disciple of Jesus, you join God's family as a child and co-heir with Christ. But it is not just you and Jesus in that family—it includes every other person on earth who chooses Jesus as well. The family of God is huge, including all who have faith in Him from the beginning of the world until now. The family of God is called the Church.

The Church covers the entire globe, and it brings all Christians together. We are united in the same faith and part of the same body. We do not look, speak, dress, or act the same way. We do not have the same interests in movies, books, or media. We are not of the same age, ethnicity, or gender. None of this matters, however, because we are all united in Christ. Jesus is the head of the Church who directs the path of His people. We have all died to our sins and look forward to an eternal life with God. We all have the same Spirit that dwells within us, guiding us to faithfulness. Because we are all unified under Christ, the Church is one family that loves God and each other.

Just like a human body, the Church is made of many parts. God celebrates diversity in the fact that we are all uniquely gifted by Him. As members of the Church body, we are called to serve. Can you imagine if your stomach decided to stop digesting food because it was sad it was not a hand that got to write? Or if your foot decided to stop stepping because it wanted to be an arm that could throw? God created you for a specific purpose within the body, and He is glorified when you serve in the way He made you. For our human bodies to function well, we need each and every part to work as God designed. The same is true of the Church. God, through the power of the Spirit, gives each believer spiritual gifts. When we all exercise the gifts given to us, the Church functions as intended. Through our service in the body, we are exemplifying the Lord and advancing His kingdom.

When you become a disciple of Jesus, you join God's family as a child and co-heir with Christ.

God celebrates diversity
IN THE FACT THAT
WE ARE ALL UNIQUELY
GIFTED BY HIM.

REFLECT REFLECT REFLECT REFLECT

What is the Church?

_____
_____
_____
_____
_____
_____

How can you serve your local church?

_____
_____
_____
_____
_____
_____

Why do you need to be a part of the Church?
Find someone at your local church to discuss these
needs with. If you don't have a church, find a local
Bible-believing church that you can start attending.

_____
_____
_____
_____
_____
_____
_____
_____

AMBASSADOR TO THE WORLD

READ 2 CORINTHIANS 5:17–21; 1 PETER 2:9–10

What do you want to be when you grow up? It can feel like we are plagued by this question from the moment we learn to speak. As little kids, we start out with confident answers like fireman, ballerina, or astronaut. But often, as we get older, we start to question our path. Most of us want to work with purpose and know that what we are doing matters. This desire is good because we were created for a specific purpose: to be ambassadors for God.

An ambassador is someone sent by a nation, maybe a king, to be a representative in the world. Kings often sent ambassadors to foreign nations with a message or to accomplish a goal. They were given the king's authority to speak on behalf of the monarchy. Other nations would look to the ambassador of a country to determine what a king was really like. For example, if the ambassador was intelligent and kind, it was assumed the king was the same. Because of this weighty responsibility, ambassadors were specifically chosen by the monarch himself.

If you follow Jesus, it is because God adopted you into His family. He chose you. And everyone God chooses to save becomes a new creation and is sent out into the world with a new job as an ambassador for Christ. As ambassadors, we are God's representatives to the world. We are given the power of the Holy Spirit to share the gospel with authority. The world will look at how we speak and act in order to understand who our King is. That might feel like a great responsibility and a job you probably do not feel equipped to do. Just as we cannot do enough good works to save ourselves, we cannot be ambassadors for God on our own. God saves us through His own power, and He then equips us to live as new creations. Paul explains how God equips us to live when he writes, "I am sure of this, that He who started a good work in you will carry it on to completion until the day of Christ Jesus" (Philippians 1:6). God gives us a weighty purpose in this world, but He also prepares us daily to accomplish it.

The New Testament is filled with books called the Epistles, or letters, to the early churches in Europe and Asia. These letters were sent to the first ambassadors for Jesus to tell them how to fulfill their new role. As you read the books between Acts and Revelation, you will begin to understand how God asks His new creations to live. Our ultimate purpose in life is to love God and love others. God's Word is a guide on how to do that best. We are chosen and set apart for the purpose of loving this world in the name of Jesus. However, we are not on our own in this mission. God sent the Holy Spirit to dwell within us and the people of the Church to surround us as we work.

As ambassadors, we are God's representatives to the world.

We are chosen
AND SET APART
FOR THE PURPOSE OF
LOVING THIS WORLD IN
THE NAME OF JESUS.

How do you feel about God giving you the role
of His ambassador to the world?

_____

_____

_____

_____

_____

_____

What is one thing you can do this week
to be an ambassador for Jesus?

_____

_____

_____

_____

_____

Read Colossians 3:23. How can you work for
God rather than for others or yourself?

_____

_____

_____

_____

_____

_____

_____

SABBATH

What is rest? How do you have it?
Take a minute and answer those questions below.

_____

_____

_____

Usually, we rest by either sleeping or zoning out. Sleep is good for our bodies and souls; zoning out is distracting and ends up leaving us more tired. We zone out by watching TV, browsing the internet or social media for hours at a time, or playing video games through the night. None of these things are bad, but they are also not exactly restful because they tend to overstimulate our brains and emotions rather than create peace. So how do we rest?

First, we must recognize that God is the Creator of rest. He created the garden of Eden to be a place of perfect rest, and He rested from His work on the seventh day (Genesis 2:1–3). But when Adam and Eve chose their own way over God's perfect design, they lost the perfect rest they once enjoyed. Now, their work became burdensome, and they grew tired. The rest for which God created them was disrupted.

Generations later, God commanded His people to keep a Sabbath, a set-apart day of rest each week (Exodus 20:8–11). He gave them the Sabbath for their own well-being but also to point them to their need for true rest, the kind of rest that could only come from Him. The Sabbath was merely a shadow of the perfect rest for which humanity was created.

Jesus Christ came to restore our rest. In His earthly ministry, He reminded people that "the Sabbath was made for man and not man for the Sabbath" (Mark 2:27). He taught them that He is the Lord of the Sabbath. Jesus is our one true source of rest.

Jesus Christ came to restore our rest.

So, how can we truly rest? We can rest by turning to Jesus. In Him, we no longer have to endlessly labor or toil, for He offers true rest for all who come to Him (Matthew 11:28–30). He also promises to bring us into an eternity of rest in the new heaven and new earth (Revelation 21:1–22:5).

We can rest by turning to Jesus.

While we are not required to practice the Sabbath like the ancient Israelites were, we can still benefit from regular, intentional time spent resting in our Savior's presence. Our God loves us so much that He wants us to take a break. When we choose to rest in His presence rather than work endlessly, we show God and the rest of the world that we trust Him to take care of us, so we do not need to stress about taking care of ourselves.

Find a time this week when you can rest. Consider asking your family to rest with you. Consider what things in your life feel like work or a burden, and put those things aside for the day. Try to stay away from devices if you can. Instead, go on a walk, have lunch with a friend or family member, or read a book that teaches you more about Jesus. Spend time in prayer and with your Bible. You might be surprised how peaceful and joyful you feel at the end of the day.

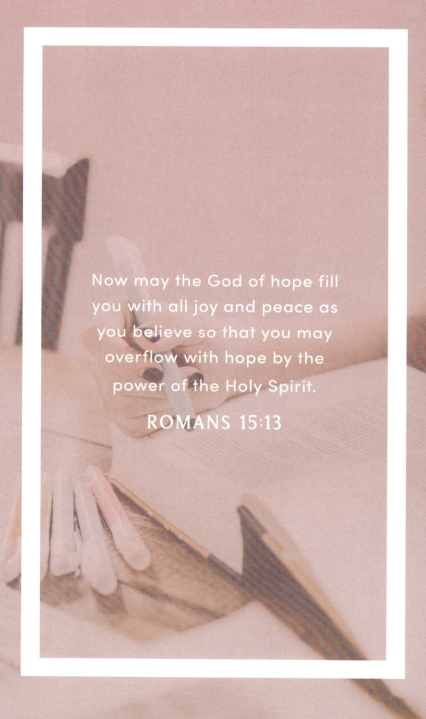

Now may the God of hope fill you with all joy and peace as you believe so that you may overflow with hope by the power of the Holy Spirit.

ROMANS 15:13

WHAT NOW?

You did it! It is an amazing accomplishment to complete a study like this, especially if it is your first time. Take a moment to thank God for what He has taught you through the course of this study, and feel proud of your faithfulness each step of the way. Hopefully, this is just the beginning of intentionally growing your relationship with God.

Now is the time to figure out your next steps. Spending time with God should be a daily habit by now, but it can easily slip out of your schedule if it is not prioritized. If you are not sure where to go next, look through more studies from The Daily Grace Co.® to guide you; you can find these at thedailygraceco.com. If you want to read the Bible on your own, consider reading one of the Gospels (Matthew, Mark, Luke, or John). If you have other friends who want to study the Word as well, pick a book you can all read together. That way, you can ask questions and learn from one another. If you are not part of a local church yet, find one. That is where you will grow the most and find others to live and serve alongside. Above all else, love God and love others.

We pray that you would find peace, joy, hope, and truth in God's Word and that you would continue to study it day after day, year after year, until God calls you home. You are deeply loved by a perfect God who wants to be near you always. He has come close to us in Jesus Christ so that you, too, can come close to Him.

We pray that you would find peace, joy, hope, and truth in God's Word.

BIBLIOGRAPHY

Bergen, Robert D. "Genesis." In *Christian Standard Study Bible*, edited by Edwin A. Blum and Trevin Wax, 1–86. Nashville: Holman Bible Publishers, 2017.

Blaising, Craig A. "Christ in the Old Testament." In *Christian Standard Study Bible*, edited by Edwin A. Blum and Trevin Wax, xli-xlvii. Nashville: Holman Bible Publishers, 2017.

Dingfelder, Sadie. "Psychologist Testifies on the Risks of Solitary Confinement." *Monitor on Psychology*. American Psychological Association. October 2012. https://www.apa.org/monitor/2012/10/solitary#:~:text=As%20a%20result%20of%20the,some%20suffer%20hallucinations%2C%20he%20said.

Guthrie, George H. "How to Read and Study the Bible." In *Christian Standard Study Bible*, edited by Edwin A. Blum and Trevin Wax, xli-xlvii. Nashville: Holman Bible Publishers, 2017.

Hallesby, Ole. *Prayer.* Translated by Clarence J. Carlsen. Minneapolis: Augsburg Fortress, 1994.

Heideman, Jennie, Alli McDougal, and Helen Hummel, ed. *The Bible Themes Handbook.* Hanover, MD: The Daily Grace Co., 2022

Hess, Alexa. *Rest from Eden to Eternity.* Hanover, MD: The Daily Grace Co., 2022.

Kaiser, Walter C. "Jesus in the Old Testament." *Gordon Conwell Theological Seminary Blog.* Gordon Conwell Theological Seminary. August 9, 2011. https://www.gordonconwell.edu/blog/jesus-in-the-old-testament/

Kitchen, Kenneth A. "The Historical Reliability of the Old Testament." In *Christian Standard Study Bible*, edited by Edwin A. Blum and Trevin Wax, xli-xlvii. Nashville: Holman Bible Publishers, 2017.

Krueger, Michael. "Self-Authenticating Scripture." June 3, 2019. Produced by Ligonier Ministries. 1:17. https://www.youtube.com/watch?v=t2aIUvB12g4.

Piper, John. "Children, Heirs, and Fellow Sufferers." April 21, 2002. Produced by Desiring God. 41:52. https://www.desiringgod.org/messages/children-heirs-and-fellow-sufferers.

Piper, John. "How Do I Pray the Bible?" February 6, 2017. Produced by Desiring God. 11:14. https://www.desiringgod.org/interviews/how-do-i-pray-the-bible.

Piper, John. "How Do We Pray in the Spirit?" August 2, 2021. Produced by Desiring God. 10:54. https://www.desiringgod.org/interviews/how-do-we-pray-in-the-spirit.

Sowerby, Tracy. "The Role of the Ambassador and the Use of Ciphers." *State Papers Online*. 1509-1714. Cengage Learning EMEA Ltd., 2009. https://www.gale.com/intl/essays/tracy-sowerby-role-ambassador-use-ciphers.

Sproul, R.C. and Robert Wolgemuth. *What's in the Bible: The Story of God through Time and Eternity.* 2000.

Strauss, Mark L. *Four Portraits, One Jesus: A Survey of Jesus and the Gospels.* Grand Rapids: Zondervan Academic, 2020.

Tyndale. "The Difference Between Literal and Dynamic Translations of the Bible." *Tyndale Stories.* https://www.tyndale.com/stories/literal-translation-vs-paraphrase-of-the-bible.

Whitney, Don. "What Are Spiritual Disciplines?" December 31, 2015. Produced by Desiring God. 8:09. https://www.desiringgod.org/interviews/what-are-spiritual-disciplines.

Thank you for studying God's Word with us!